How to Develop Advanced Psychic Abilities

Obtain Information about the Past, Present and Future Through Clairvoyance

Sophia diGregorio

Other Books by Sophia diGregorio:

Practical Black Magic: How to Hex and Curse Your Enemies

Traditional Witches' Formulary and Potion-making Guide: Recipes for Magical Oils, Powders and Other Potions

How to Write Your Own Spells for Any Purpose and Make Them Work

What's Next After Wicca? Non-Wiccan Occult Practices and Traditional Witchcraft by Sophia diGregorio

Grimoire of Santa Muerte: Spells and Rituals of Most Holy Death, the Unofficial Saint of Mexico (Santa Muerte Series) (Volume 1)

Grimoire of Santa Muerte, Vol. 2: Altars, Meditations, Divination and Witchcraft Rituals for Devotees of Most Holy Death (Santa Muerte Series) (Volume 2)

The Occult Files of Sophia diGregorio Bitcoin and Altcoins Patronage Program: How to Join Our Cryptocurrency-Based Patronage Program and Why We are Doing Things This Way

Traditional Witches' History of the Occult Banking System: How Witches and Occultists Can Use Bitcoin and Altcoins for Privacy and Anti-Discrimination by Sophia diGregorio

The Occult Files of Sophia diGregorio: The Public Monologues of 2018

How to Develop Advanced Psychic Abilities

Obtain Information about the Past, Present and Future Through Clairvoyance

Sophia diGregorio

2019

Winter Tempest Books

How to Develop Advanced Psychic Abilities: Obtain Information about the Past, Present and Future Through Clairvoyance.

Copyright © 2019 Sophia diGregorio

All rights reserved.

ISBN: 1-949999-02-5
ISBN-13:978-1-949999-02-0

This is the first paperback edition of this book. The ebook edition of it was originally published by Winter Tempest Books on April 12, 2012.

Cover Image: Andreagrossmann / John William Waterhouse, The Crystal Ball, Wikimediacommons.org

License statement: This document contains material protected under copyright laws. Any unauthorized reprint, transmission or resale of this material without the express permission of the author is strictly prohibited. No part of this book may be used or reproduced in any manner whatsoever without written permission from the author except in the case of brief quotations embodied in critical articles and reviews.

Contents

Chapter 1	Introduction	1
Chapter 2	Esoteric Science	5
Chapter 3	Types of Psychic Experience	11
Chapter 4	Spontaneous Development of Advanced Psychic Abilities	25
Chapter 5	Detoxifying and Stimulating the Glandular and Nervous Systems	31
Chapter 6	The Psychic Diet	39
Chapter 7	Meditation Techniques for Advanced Psychic Development	43
Chapter 8	Herbs, Crystals, and Potions	49
Chapter 9	Tools and Methods for Advanced Psychic Development	53
Chapter 10	Journaling and Keeping Records	69
Chapter 11	Pitfalls to Be Aware Of	73

Chapter 12	Signs that Your Abilities are Developing	77
Chapter 13	Final Words of Encouragement	79
	References	81
	Bibliography	83

Chapter 1
Introduction

What are Advanced Psychic Abilities?

Advanced psychic abilities help us to live fuller, more aware lives. They set human beings apart from the animals and, when they function at a high level, they enable us to achieve that which seems beyond the ordinary. Great artists, composers, and inventors all make use of them. Such abilities are a complex faculty involving the use of the whole mind on different planes or frequencies to receive explicit information through clairvoyance, clairaudience, and claircognizance.

These abilities are not the same as instinct or "gut feeling," which is a lower response that comes from the more animal side of man. Nor are they empathy, which is the ability to feel what others feel. Such abilities all come from the lower chakra centers, in particular the solar plexus and while they are important, they are often vague or of no discernible meaning.

Clairvoyance or "clear seeing" is the power to see what is ordinarily hidden. This function is associated with the mind and the energy centers of the head, in particular the third eye, which is located in the region of the pineal gland. Clairvoyance is sometimes accompanied by clairaudience or "clear hearing," which is the ability to hear what is normally inaudible.

Sometimes psychics receive information very directly without being able to determine if it is the product of clairaudience or clairvoyance. In such cases, a "download" of information is received from some outside source. This is called "claircognizance," which is the ability to simply know something by other than ordinary means, although it may not be clear where the information came from.

These higher intuitive functions may or may not be accompanied by the lower response of emotion, empathy, or instinct. While the experiences are not mutually exclusive, they are very different psychic abilities.

Most people have experienced the lower forms of psychic ability. For example, they may have followed up on a hunch that turned out to be right, or they may have experienced a sense of foreboding before an unpleasant event. But the majority of people do not see vivid pictures in their minds pertaining to something other than their own memories or imagination, or hear voices other than their own inner monologue.

Furthermore, people who injudiciously admit to such things have been ridiculed, persecuted, and even institutionalized. Although many people who possess such abilities benefit themselves and others in many different ways.

What Can Be Done with Advanced Psychic Abilities?

Accessing information through extraordinary means is more than just an idle pastime or a symptom of eccentricity. The ability can enable people to do many remarkable things.

The famous clairvoyant Edgar Cayce, known as "the sleeping prophet" for his ability to act as a medium while in a sleep-like trance, gave very specific information to his individual patients including remedies for their specific health problems and descriptions of their past lives. From these readings, information about natural remedies, the power of colors, stones, herbs, and the history of the earth as far back as Atlantis have been compiled. The information that Edgar Cayce obtained in this way proved to be useful to many people besides his original patients.

Other famous mystics, whose visions have impacted the world, include St. John of Patmos, who is the author of the *Book of Revelations,* Nostradamus, Joseph Smith, Aleister Crowley, and the Theosophists Madame Helena P. Blavatsky, Annie Besant, and C.W. Leadbeater whose work strongly influenced the modern New Age movement.

Information obtained by extraordinary means has profoundly affected the way we live our everyday lives. For example, Nikola Tesla, who invented alternating current, radio, and other forms of wireless transmission had detailed visions of his inventions. He worked out the mechanics of new devices entirely in his mind before he attempted to create them physically.

The best work of artists, writers, and musicians is inspired, as if it came from a place outside themselves. Visions, sounds, and thoughts flow into their minds and combine with their natural talents to create something extraordinary in the physical world.

Some writers even attribute the authorship of their books to the spirits from whom they came. Annie Besant attributed some of her best work to the spirit Djwhal Khul. The series of books, commonly referred to as "the Seth material," was attributed to a spirit who spoke through Jane Roberts. By means of information first received through a Ouija board, Pearl Curran became the medium for the spirit of Patience Worth, to whom she attributed the authorship of several novels and poems.

Advanced psychic abilities have long been used to find hidden mineral reserves and sources of water. They are used to locate missing items and sometimes missing people. On occasion, police departments have used psychics to solve difficult cases.

Some healers use their clairvoyant abilities to diagnose abnormalities of internal organs and use this information to help their patients. The physical bodies of living beings, including humans and animals, can be penetrated with etheric vision, so that the inner workings of organs and systems of the body can be seen.

These are only a few examples because there is really no limit to the information that can be obtained through advanced psychic abilities, which we can use to help ourselves and others.

SOPHIA DIGREGORIO

Chapter 2
Esoteric Science

The true science that explains the nature of our world is an esoteric one, which is based on the concept of vibrational harmonics and frequency ranges. It is often at odds with modern official science and, therefore, it is subject to ridicule by its adherents.

Esoteric science says that all things in physical existence are atomic and necessarily of a binary (or dual) nature. Like a battery, an atom has an energetic polarity that can be described as positive or negative, male or female, one or null, etc. This is what is meant by "duality" or the dual nature of the universe that is talked about, although not often understood in many New Age circles.

This atomic inequality or lack of equilibrium, within the electromagnetically charged nucleus of the atom, is what causes vibration. So, all things that appear solid are actually in a perpetual state of motion. If they ceased to be in motion, they would cease to exist in the dual universe, which is all that we would regard as both physical or spiritual in nature.

Everything that exists in either the physical plane or any other in the dual universe emanates a wave or frequency. Objects and organisms produce their own unique, vibrational harmonic signature.

We live in a sea of these emanations, which exist in a vast etheric field, through which their signals pass. These signals can be likened to the frequency received by your satellite dish as it transmits images through a processor to your television screen.

Similar to a digital satellite signal processor, the human mind is capable of receiving and interpreting signals to form pictures and sounds. For example, the retina of the physical eye is capable of intercepting the signals of a small section of vibratory frequencies. This is the ordinary visible light spectrum. In exactly the same way, the human eardrum is capable of receiving a similar range of sound vibrations.

But there is an infinite number of frequencies above and below the range most human beings can see and hear. Some of these are the frequency ranges at which radio, television, satellite signals, and microwaves function. We know they are there. We use the technology. But we cannot hear or see them.

Furthermore, people possess varying abilities to intercept and interpret the normally perceptible physical range of frequencies. For example, there are people who do not see the same thing when their eyes and brains process the frequencies that create color. These people are called "color blind" because they do not see what most other people see. Not everyone has the same audio range, either. Some people are incapable of hearing tones within the normal physical range. Furthermore, there are people who are more sensitive to the range of frequencies that produce sound and vision.

Perhaps even more pertinent to advanced psychic abilities, there are people who are more sensitive to electromagnetic frequencies than others. Such people may experience headaches and respiratory difficulties when exposed to high electromagnetic frequencies.

Some forms of advanced psychic ability may simply be an extension of the human mind's more ordinary abilities because our bodies exist on frequencies outside the physical ranges. We have extended bodies of subtler energetic form on an infinite number of frequencies. So, the eyes and ears, also, exist on other planes and are capable of receiving transmissions within that range, as well.

You experience the vibratory world around you every second of every day, usually without thinking about it, however, if you have ever sensed that someone was looking at your back and turned around to find someone staring at you, you have intercepted and interpreted these subtle frequencies emanating from the mind and body of another person.

The Frequency Ranges or Planes

According to the Theosophists, who have provided very good models and descriptive terms for the exploration of all kinds of esoteric subjects, there are many degrees of fineness of the frequency ranges of the body, which they call "planes" of existence.

The following list represents the human body from its densest to its subtlest form.

1. Physical body (the common five-sense reality to which we have been conditioned)
2. Nervous system
3. Glandular system of the physical body
4. Chakra system
5. Etheric body
6. Mental body
7. Auric (emotional) body
8. Infinite planes (or bandwidths of frequencies of increasingly finer substance)

These bodies and systems are not distinct or separate from one another, but interpenetrating and interconnected. Furthermore, while the above conceptualization helps in understanding some of these terms and ideas, it is necessarily imperfect. This is just a way to apply language to ideas that are outside the field of ordinary experience, so that we can discuss and study this esoteric subject.

The force that gives life to the body on all of its planes of existence is a kind of electromagnetic energy called "life force" and other names, which is dual (binary) in nature. It is this polarity that causes the vibration. Again, this applies to all of the planes. Therefore, those more subtle planes, such as the auric, are of the same dual nature as the physical. They just vibrate at a frequency outside our normal, conditioned reality.

This life force, which animates the cells of man and everything around us, is also called the "ether" or "quintessence" (fifth element) in esoteric parlance. When a signal or frequency passes from one place to another, it travels through the "dynamic ether," which is not dead space as perceived by the official science at different times. Everything in the duality of our existence vibrates because of its binary nature and nothing is dead or empty.

People who are in tune with these frequencies can sense and manipulate them, as in the case of so-called "miracle" healing. Of course, it is not miraculous, at all, it only requires an understanding of this esoteric science and knowledge of how to manipulate the fields involved.

Conversely, knowledge of these fields can be used to harm people. Traditionally, this has been done by black magicians, although in recent decades, mind manipulating technology has emerged creating a growing problem referred to as "electronic harassment."

Perpetrators of this kind of harassment use frequency generating technology to target a particular person on the basis of their individual harmonic wave signature to influence their thoughts, dreams, and emotions by sending signals to the target's skull or bouncing it off the walls inside a room. Because esoteric science and occult technology is little known or accepted outside of occult circles, the target often believes he or she is going insane.

This technology, which can intercept, interpret, and transmit signals on non-physical planes mimics advanced psychic abilities in humans.

Nearest to the physical body is the etheric body, which is actually a dense, nearly physical aspect of the auric field. It is thoroughly described in the book, *The Etheric Double*, by A. E. Powell. Influencing this body can have a very fast and direct effect on the physical body. It is hypothesized that this is the body seen in cases of spirit manifestations.[1]

The five sensory organs exist on the etheric and greater astral body just as they do on the physical plane. So, even if it is latent and unused in many people, the ability to intercept and interpret signals on these different levels of frequency exists because etheric versions of these organs exist, even when their physical counterparts are missing or malfunctioning.

The astral and mental bodies are able to intercept and process signals at different densities or planes of existence, as well. The astral body is a finer density of the etheric body and interacts closely the glandular and nervous systems of the physical body. It is through the astral body and its spinning vortices (chakras or energy centers) that the body receives and maintains a supply of vital force. It, also, receives vital force from nourishment on the physical plane.

Through the function of the mental body we have the power of claircognizance, which is the ability of inexplicably knowing something through unconventional means. The mental body intercepts and interprets signals on this plane instantaneously.

It is important to remember that even at the densest physical level, that which seems solid is, in fact, vibrating at a very high speed. All matter is essentially energy and this is the case regardless of its plane of existence. This is not to say the physical or the etheric is not real, however, it is all real.

We can receive and process frequencies on those different bandwidths. This is the nature of clairvoyance, clairaudience, and other psychic abilities.

Essentially, psychics are just people who are able to intercept and interpret a broader range of frequencies than the average person. While it is not absolutely necessary to understand the esoteric science behind psychic abilities to develop and use them, it does help to show that this is a natural ability and to try to explain how it occurs.

SOPHIA DIGREGORIO

Chapter 3
Types of Psychic Experience

In order to recognize your own abilities as they develop, it is helpful to understand the different types of experiences people have. Advanced psychic abilities may manifest themselves in a variety of ways and may involve the astral, mental, etheric, and even the physical body.

Those who receive information through extraordinary sight and hearing do so both at a distance and in the nearby. They may obtain information from the past, present, or future. The experience may be very physical in nature or dream-like. Transmissions may be of a brief nature, such as a flash of insight or imagery, or it may be a longer, more complex experience, such as those that take place in sessions with mediums or in dreams.

Psychic experiences are of an infinitely broad nature and, therefore, difficult to classify. But, for the sake of this discussion, an attempt is made here to do so.

1. Clairvoyance and Clairaudience: This involves a broad range of experiences, which include seeing and hearing spirits, alien beings, shape shifters, faeries, etc. The experience may or may not be attached to a location and can include information from the past, present, and future.

2. Power of Discernment: This can manifest as a claircognizant experience, where a person simply knows something about a situation or an individual. It is, also, sometimes described as the ability to "see through" someone, to see the true nature of a person. It can include other experiences like observing what seems to be a shift in some aspect of an individual's physical appearance.

3. Flashes of Insight: These include high level forms of intuition in the form of visions, words, and phrases. These experiences are brief, but profound.

4. Dreams: These occur during R.E.M. sleep and can be vivid, colorful, and highly detailed. Precognitive dreams often have some unique characteristic of realism that lets the dreamer know it is of special significance. Some dreams seem to be a form of astral projection or out of body experience wherein part of the dreamer, in astral form, goes on a journey.

5. Trance: This is an altered state of consciousness, similar to the dream state, in which the person has enhanced mental capacity to focus and to receive information. Trance states are induced by hypnosis or self-induced through meditation or self-hypnosis. It is used in mediumship and channeling, and when performing divination.

6. Divination: During the process of divining, people consciously use their advanced psychic abilities to obtain specific information about the past, present, or future. It is possible to permanently increase your psychic abilities through the study and practice of some forms of divination.

The types of information that may be accessed by extraordinary means is without limit. For some people, the means by which they obtain information are consistently of one kind or another. But it is possible to experience a wide variety of different kinds of clairvoyance, clairaudience, and claircognizance using the different "bodies" or frequency ranges.

The Etheric Plane

Nearest the physical state, in the set of vibrational frequencies closest to the ones we commonly operate on every day, is the etheric plane. When attuned to this set of frequencies, a person might notice a change in the appearance of his or her surroundings.

For example, objects may appear transparent, thereby allowing him or her to know the contents of a locked box, the goings on in an adjacent room, or the information written in a sealed letter. The person is able to exercise the etheric faculty while still maintaining awareness of the object and its physical surroundings.

This can occur spontaneously without the person being entirely aware of what triggers it, however, in a well-developed psychic, this ability is completely under the person's control and can be employed at will.

When this faculty is exercised upon objects in the immediate surroundings, the solid ground may appear to some extent transparent, so the psychic is able to see what lies beneath it. If there is a vein of water, a source of minerals or oil beneath the surface, it can be perceived in this state of altered awareness.

Etheric sight can be applied at great distances, as well, in order to retrieve lost information.

For example, Edgar Cayce spoke of "The Hall of Records," which is alleged to be buried under the tomb of the great Sphinx of Giza in Egypt, as the source for much of his information. Its location has never been physically verified. But there are known to be other libraries[2] such as the Library of Timbuktu, which contain innumerable important manuscripts detailing the history of mankind. There are, also, areas of well-known museums and libraries that are off-limits to the general public. A psychic with a highly developed etheric faculty may be able to locate them and read their contents at a distance.

Sacred sites hold historical records in the form of an energetic imprint on the etheric field that can be read by people who are at that location.

An example of this is illustrated by the experience of a well-respected professor who visited the site of the Oracle of Delphi in Greece. She waited until the other tourists had left and sat in meditative silence amid the ruins of the temple when she heard the music and song emanating from the ether. She was not a developed psychic, but this flash of clairaudient ability gave her first hand insight into the history of this monument. And, it awakened her to further possibilities.

Certain places in the world seem to bear such a strong energetic imprint that even people who are not highly psychic have unusual experiences wherein they see a transparency of the past over the present. A very few examples of such places are El Paso, Texas, and the surrounding valley at the feet of the Guadalupe Mountains; the island of Crete in Greece; some areas of the State of Michoacán in Mexico; the North Sea off the coast of The Netherlands; and the San Fernando Valley, which surrounds Los Angeles, California.

The strong imprint around El Paso, Texas, gives many visitors visions of the town and the surrounding valley at a much earlier time, especially when it was a Mexican frontier town. It appears that this phenomenon was experienced by the country singer, Marty Robbins, who immortalized the city in a series of three songs. In one of the songs, entitled *El Paso,* he tells a story about what seems to be a past life experience. In another, entitled *El Paso City*, he asks if he lived in the City in another time. A third song, entitled *Feleena,* carries on the theme of the first one. Visitors to El Paso, also, report experiencing vivid dreams during their stay.

Greece has many relics from a staggering span of centuries, as any observant traveler to the country knows. But one visitor had an astonishing experience off the southern coast of Crete on the Red Beach near Matala. After swimming out into the water and reaching a very relaxed state, her sight shifted to the etheric and she was suddenly aware of prehistoric turtles and other large reptiles in her surroundings.

The North Sea holds a strong imprint of centuries of historic battles and lost ships. While the San Fernando Valley contains imprints from many different eras, including prehistoric ones. The Mexican State of Michoacán contains an area where the surroundings, including foliage and animals, appear prehistoric.

Although psychic experiences involving etheric sight are more common in some places than others, they can occur anywhere, especially to psychics who are attuned to these frequencies. Such experiences are similar in many ways to psychometry.

Psychometry

Psychometry is the skill of being able to touch an object and receive images or sounds that tell something about the object or the person who owned it. An extended form of psychometry may certainly play a role in many cases involving a specific location because, in these instances, people are coming into direct contact with the ground and air of a place.

There are some objects that seem to have been intended to be used for this very purpose. For example, the legendary crystal skulls are associated with all kinds of historical dreams and visions.

The most famous of these is the Mitchell-Hedges crystal skull, named after the adventurer F.A. Mitchell and his daughter Anna Le Guillon Mitchell-Hedges, who found it in 1924 while living among the Mayans of Guatemala. The skull was reportedly tested by Hewlett-Packard in 1970 and found to possess some unusual properties, in particular, it was carved on two axes in such a way that would have been impossible with the tools available at the time it was found. Furthermore, there is no sign of heat or abrasion on the crystal.[3]

People who slept near the skull or touched it reported having vivid nightmares and waking visions of what seemed to be historical events among the Mayans. This has led some people to believe that the skull was programmed for the purpose of recording and transmitting information in this fashion.

Other forms of psychometry are more ordinary and less dramatic. For example, many people are able to obtain information by simply touching an object that has a strong psychic imprint on it.

Items that are frequently worn by people carry a strong personal energetic imprint. Personal items belonging to an individual can help a psychic tune into that person's unique frequency harmonic to obtain information through clairvoyance and clairaudience.

Objects, such as weapons that have been used in the commission of a violent crime, may hold a strong imprint of that one event.

Generally, those skilled in psychometry must touch the item or hold it in their hands, however, this is not always the case. Sometimes just standing near an object or looking at it can produce vivid psychic experiences.

The Akashic Records

"Akashic records" is the term used by the early Theosophists to mean "etheric records." These records may or may not have once existed physically, but they now exist only in the etheric plane.

All of the history of the universe and human experience is contained there and can be accessed by anyone who knows how to do it. It may be seen as a universal mind with a central repository or as simply an imprint of energy on the etheric field that a person mentally tunes into.

It is most commonly accessed by psychics who go into a self-induced trance, then either retrieve the vibrational frequencies from the ether and decode them or astrally project themselves to the source of the information they desire.

Since the etheric field exists outside of time and space, it can hold information about not only the past, but the present, and the future. The etheric records may have a relationship to the experiences of claircognizance, precognition, divination, and prophetic dreams.

The fairly common experience of deja vu is a form of precognition that occurs when a person has information about an event, but doesn't recognize it until the moment that event begins to unfold. The information is stored in the person's subconscious from a vision or dream, which may be a product of the subconscious mind accessing the etheric records.

Remote Viewing

Remote viewing is a scientific-sounding name for clairvoyance, clairaudience and, in particular, the ability to project energetic aspects of one's self to a remote location. It is a specific protocol for doing so, which was devised by black operatives within the *Stargate Project* of the U.S. Federal government. The documents related to this project were declassified in 1990, and a number of the participants published books about their protocols. The *Stargate Project* is satirized in the 2009 movie, *The Men Who Stare at Goats*.

Typical remote viewing protocols involved experiments similar to those conducted at parapsychology research centers like Stanford University using objects like *Zerner* cards and dice, but frequently involved more complex and defense-related subject matter. For example, psychics were asked to view specific remote target locations in foreign countries and to mentally go into people's offices and access information from files. Participants sometimes drew sketches of what they saw.

Psychic warfare programs like *Stargate* were established by the U.S. in response to the use of esoteric scientific technology by the Soviet Union. Parapsychological studies done in the U.S.S.R were recorded by Sheila Ostrander and Lynn Schroeder in their book, *Psychic Discoveries Behind the Iron Curtain,* first published in 1970.[4]

The human mind's ability to connect with the frequencies of the various planes can be reproduced by machines, radionics machines for example, using a subtle form of electricity and radio waves. The government's use of esoteric science is not limited to the use of psychics in experiments, but has expanded into the use of wave technology.

Psychic warfare involves both intelligence gathering and mind control technology. Just like the more common occult practice of using extrasensory perception, the technological counterpart can be used to obtain information or "intelligence." Similar technology can be used to psychically attack or influence the mind of another using radiation, microwaves and extra low frequency (E.L.F.) waves.

Esoteric science is the basis for other technology, much of which is unknown to the general public.

Out of Body Experiences

Out of body experiences (O.B.E.s) are any experience in which your etheric or astral body leaves your physical body. This can occur spontaneously or willfully. In these cases, your consciousness is contained in the projected body, while the physical body remains in a state of repose.

Astral projection involves a shift in the consciousness to the astral body, which then connects to other planes of existence. The quality of these experiences can be dream-like, but very realistic, as well. In some research experiments, this effect is achieved through sensory deprivation, involving prolonged stays in a darkened, silent chamber. Although it is uncertain how effective this method may be. The fact is that O.B.E.s frequently involve diminished physical sensory perception and sometimes temporary physical paralysis.

Some types of astral projection involve lucid dreaming, in which the person is aware that they are dreaming and is able to control what happens in the dream. Such dreams are characterized by very detailed, realistic images, and vivid colors. Places and faces may be very distinct and recognizable. One of the most enjoyable experiences lucid dreamers commonly report is the sensation of flying and actually soaring over the tops of trees and buildings. These experiences are sometimes so vivid that, upon awakening, dreamers have to convince themselves that it really was a dream.

Astral or etheric projection is consciously practiced by some healers who go into a trance state and leave their bodies to locate the physical body of a person to be healed. There, they conduct their healing sessions on the subject as if they were physically present. This same technique is used by healers in self-healing, wherein they leave their physical bodies to perform their own healing as if they were two separate entities. This technique is described in the book, *Magical Healing: How to Heal Yourself and Others with Your Mind*, by Angela Kaelin.

O.B.E.s sometimes occur spontaneously, not only in cases of dreaming, but in the case of severe trauma. People who survive violent crimes, such as rape or attempted murder, report having left their body during the course of the attack that nearly took their lives. This seems to be an act of cosmic mercy, so that the person is removed from the horror and pain of the situation, at least, temporarily. Commonly, such experiences involve the sense of hovering above their bodies and witnessing what is happening in a detached way.

Projections of the etheric body, sometimes called doppelgängers, can be seen or felt by some people. In cases involving psychic attack, unshielded attackers or their astral or etheric minions may be perceived by clairvoyant victims. They may appear either as shadowy beings or as distinct, apparently physical beings either in clear waking visions or in dreams.

Some spiritual adepts are able to consciously project their etheric bodies to other locations with such a density that it can easily be seen, spoken to, and even touched by others, while their actual physical body remains in another location lying in a state of repose or a posture of meditation. Many saints and yogis are said to have this ability, which is sometimes called bi-location.

One of the most recently living saints to display this ability was St. Padre Pio (1887-1968), who appeared in apparent physical form to people in order to perform healing, say words of comfort, give Last Rites, or perform other duties, while his physical body was in another place. Other famous saints with this ability include St. Antony of Padua, the Comte de St. Germaine, and St. Martin de Porres.

In India, bi-location is one of the siddhis or "accomplishments" of adepts. When Babaji was living in India, many people claimed that he came to visit them at their homes and asked them to come to him. Some of these people said they had never heard of him before his visitation.

Angels, Guardians, and Spiritual Guides

Historically, there are many instances of visitations from angels and other benevolent spirits. Angels are said to be messengers of god, who give information to people, sometimes whispering in a person's ear, at other times appearing in etheric form.

Some accounts involve life-saving aid rendered by angels in hazardous situations. In these cases, angels are able to have an effect on physical matter, for example, stopping a car accident or rendering advice or aid to people in need. Angels seem to be capable of manifesting in very physical ways and have the ability to change their appearance, so it is said that we may be unaware that they are among us.

At other times, the appearance of these beings of light is more subtle. They provide a soothing and comforting presence in the household and surround and comfort the dying. They are, also, employed to guard people and possessions and keep them safe from harm.

Some beings of light may actually be an aspect of ourselves or what is called the "higher self." This is the part of us that acts as a messenger or medium between the physical frequencies and the non-physical ones. In some cases of mediumship, it appears that the medium's "control" or messenger is, in fact, his or her own higher self.

Other communications, which have yielded very important information to occultists, involve highly advanced spiritual beings sometimes called the Secret Chiefs, the Great White Brotherhood, or the Ascended Masters. An example of one of these beings is Djwhal Khul, who telepathically dictated important esoteric information to the Theosophist and author Alice Bailey.

Spiritual guardians may be seen by clairvoyants. These beings are fierce protectors of their charges.

For instance, some American Indian burial grounds are guarded by ancestral spirits whose job is to protect it from intruders. African ancestral gods, similar in appearance to the Orishas, are sometimes employed as personal guardians and may be seen standing behind practitioners of African-based religions.

In India, beings similar in description to angels are called "devas," which is Sanskrit for "brilliant light beings." The term is, also, used to mean "nature spirits" or "deities." Just like the angels of the West, devas have never had physical bodies and are spirits in the service of mankind.

Ghosts

Raps, ghostly noises and the activities of poltergeists come to our physical awareness from the etheric plane. If the manifestation from the etheric plane is strong enough, almost anyone will be able to see or hear it. Although there are some people who seem incapable of seeing or hearing anything outside the established normal frequency range.

Ghosts manifest themselves in photographs and moving film by forming out of the ether. Sometimes they appear as distinctly recognizable, although ghostly, images. More often, they manifest as orbs, which are balls of etheric energy. If psychics are present during these manifestations, they are able to communicate with the spirits associated with the orbs and may physically feel their presence, which has a similar sensation to static electricity in the air.

Etheric matter called ectoplasm is a thick vapor, intentionally formed by mediums and, somewhat, by sitters at séances where there are physical manifestations. It is the material used by spirits to form their bodies, sounds, and sometimes inanimate objects, during materialization. Once fully formed, these spirits are as apparently solid and physical as anyone else in the room and they are able to physically interact and communicate with the sitters.

Similar types of occurrences at séances, which involve the etheric field, include the appearance of a ghostly face over the medium's face; inexplicable noises, such as the loud slamming of doors where there are no doors; electrical or battery-operated equipment problems; and cold spots in the room as the energy to produce these physical manifestations is absorbed by the entities.

Generally, the medium and the sitters help the spirit to generate etheric matter needed to materialize, although some spirits are capable of doing this on their own.

Modern ghost hunters generally recognize three types of ghostly hauntings: Poltergeist; Intelligent; and Residual. Poltergeists are noisy ghosts who cause objects to move. Intelligent hauntings are those in which it is possible to interact with the spirits and received clairvoyant and clairaudient communications. Residual hauntings involve an etheric imprint of some event that plays out repeatedly, sometimes at a certain time of day.

The first two types of hauntings usually provide the best sources of information about people and things, but even residual hauntings tell something about what has taken place at a particular location.

Shape Shifters

Certain types of clairaudient and clairvoyant experiences involve entities that seem to shift frequency ranges, pop in and out of sight quickly, or transform themselves.

One of the most common types of these experiences, which is experienced by many people who do not necessarily consider themselves to be psychic, is the unidentified flying object (U.F.O.) sighting or anomalous lights in the sky. Sometimes an object moves into view and back out in a way that makes it seem to completely disappear.

One explanation for the sudden appearance and disappearance of these crafts is the shifting of frequency ranges from the physical frequency ranges to the etheric ones. In such a case, the object would appear, then disappear just as quickly.

Some people have up close encounters with beings that are outside the ordinary human experience. These experiences vary widely and some of them are very frightening for people because often the beings have some capabilities they do not understand. For instance, in the case of some abduction experiences, people report being taken out of their bedrooms through walls and ceilings. Of course, it would not be possible to take a physical body through a solid wall, but if the vibrational frequency of the body is altered to the etheric state, then this could conceivably happen.

Some beings are able to shift their appearance, often from something human to inhuman and back, again. Although, in some instances, it seems that it is the observer's frequency range that shifts, allowing him or her to see what others cannot. This apparent change in form may last for only a second, and sometimes for a minute or more. It is sometimes accompanied by a clairaudient experience, in which a psychic is able to hear what is at the fore of the being's mind or obtain some other information about it.

Shape shifters are not just part of modern U.F.O. culture, they are part of ancient lore, in which creatures such as mermaids, werewolves, and demi-gods are able to change their appearance. According to ancient legends, fairies, gnomes, and elves live in places in the earth or realms, which can only be perceived under certain conditions, either involving a shift in the frequency of the observer or the landscape. Some U.F.O. researchers believe that there is a relationship between these beings of ancient lore and modern experiences with extra-terrestrial or inner-terrestrial life forms.

If these beings of ancient lore do not exist in physical form today, they may have existed at one time and some visions of them may represent events that happened in the past. It is, also, possible that the frequency range of humans or the range of these beings shifted at one point in time, so that we no longer commonly co-exist on the same plane. Therefore, the beings can only be seen by some people under certain circumstances.

People with advanced psychic abilities may see all kinds of beings, including both angels of light and fallen angels. The term, "angels of light," is used because these beings radiate a bright light. By contrast, fallen angels are more etherically dense, dark-appearing entities. They can appear human-like, but can shift their appearance into something very ugly and almost alien-looking.

Psychics who are able to look through to see the essence of others have seen these entities in people and have seen full shifts of them, where they go from human to demonic in appearance and back again. This happens more often when the entity is angry or sexually aroused. Nightclub dancers commonly report seeing these shifts occur among men in the audience.

These beings are complex and seem to be related to the legendary fallen angels who, according to the *Book of Enoch*, chose brides from among human women. These beings were supposed to be servants to mankind, but they consider themselves superior and refused to be subordinate to man. They do not like humanity and seem to harbor a special hatred for women. They are lustful, angry, violent entities and may be at the core of some violent physical attacks on women and children.

Dark Entities

Dark entities include the aforementioned manifestations of shadowy, demonic or alien-looking beings, who typically harbor malice toward human beings, along with a broader energetic range of such entities.

Psychics can see and sometimes hear frightening entities, which seem to be around or to infest certain people and places. These dark, demonic entities, sometimes appear in the light as shadows where there is an absence of any means of casting a shadow. Alternatively, they may appear as black shadows in an already darkened room. Such an entity's voice may sound like multiple raspy voices speaking in unison. In the case of an infestation, the tramping of little feet may be heard as they scamper around the house.

The dark entities, called the "black hat man" and the "old hag," are commonly experienced by many people, especially in childhood. Typically, the vivid shadow of a man wearing a black hat or a bent, old woman will enter a child's bedroom and terrorize them with their presence, which is universally described as radiating evil. Often, the child is paralyzed with fear. The beings will remain until the child's parent comes into the room or the light is turned on.

People who over-consume alcohol are subject to infestation or possession by dark entities. At other times, obsessive entities are seen around the person. Such entities, sometimes called "alcohol entities," are seen by psychics as peering over the victim's shoulders and looking out through their eyes. Such people often display erratic, violent, or criminal behavior at the time of their obsession or possession.

Drug users open themselves up to possession by all kinds of dark entities. Many users of drugs, like crystal meth, report seeing demonic entities or even being attacked by them. People who use these drugs often appear hollow-eyed and energetically dead-looking, as if their life energy is depleted.

Organic portals are common subjects of infestation by different entities. Such people are inclined to possession by all kinds of entities and walk-in spirits. People who are organic portals usually do not display advanced psychic abilities, lack empathy, and are incapable of a full range of human emotions, although they know they are supposed to have them and will often do their best to fake it.

When they are questioned, many people who are possessed or obsessed and those who are organic portals know something isn't quite right. Often they know they have possessive and obsessive entities, but they're all right with it. They may believe they have more than one soul dwelling within their bodies. Psychologists typically recognize these people as sociopaths or psychopaths. They represent an uncomfortably large percentage of the population, especially in some geographical areas.

Black-eyed people and, in particular, black-eyed children are another strange sight. In this case, the entire eye area will be seen as a black shadow. Commonly, such people are criminals who steal or commit violent acts. The black eyes may only be seen once for a brief moment upon the initial encounter, but the psychic knows that this is a dangerous entity. This experience may, also, be accompanied by clairaudience, so that the psychic hears the foremost thoughts of the person and knows what they are about to do.

It is both a gift and a curse to be able to see dark entities and recognize those who are possessed or obsessed by them. Encounters with such people can be a little frightening, but psychics who can see them are forewarned and have a better chance of removing themselves from danger. Whereas, those who cannot see them are more at risk for becoming victims of their violence, con artistry, or other crimes.

Many of the aforementioned experiences are very common, even among people who do not consider themselves to be psychic.

SOPHIA DIGREGORIO

Chapter 4
Spontaneous Development of Advanced Psychic Abilities

As remarkable as some of the previously mentioned abilities and experiences may sound, if you are able to talk to a cross-section of the population in an open, non-judgmental setting, you will probably find that almost everyone has had an anomalous experience of some kind, at least, once in their lives.

Most people have had some experience they cannot explain. Some people have them repeatedly and those who do, typically, spend a lot of time trying to understand what they've experienced.

Interestingly, it is a vocal minority who, for some reason, seem to be incapable of ever seeing anything outside the ordinary range of the five senses, just as some people are unable to hear certain pitches or process the vibrational frequencies of colors the same way. Perhaps this has something to do with the personal frequency range within which they operate.

Understandably, many of these people are highly skeptical and can be combative toward those who have a broader range of sensory perception. But their inability to perceive anything outside the common range may well be regarded as a disability just like any other form of impaired vision or hearing.

Fortunately, the vast majority of people already have some kind of extra-sensory perception. For them, developing advanced psychic abilities is simply a matter of expanding on the abilities they already possess.

Heredity

It may be that the ability or inability to interpret frequencies beyond the common five sense range is hereditary. Every person has their own individual frequency harmonic, which is unique to them. It may be that these differences are what allow people to perceive the energy fields in their surroundings in a different way.

Different tribes and families of people have similar frequency harmonics, as well. Maybe this is why so many people of Celtic descent, even when far removed from their country of origin, tell of seeing fairies and other elemental entities associated with the forests and gardens of Ireland.

Perhaps it is why families of people, from one generation to the next, purport to have abilities traditionally ascribed to witches or seers. U.F.O. experiencers, also, report that they are visited and abducted from one generation to the next.

When psychic abilities run in families, they are often similar in nature. For example, if a mother is a natural healer, so is the daughter; if a father is visited by extra-terrestrials, so is the son; if a grandparent has the gift of second sight through dreams and waking visions, so does the grandchild. These abilities may be present from early childhood or develop later in life.

Whenever a child comes into this world with a caul, it is commonly believed that he or she will naturally have highly developed psychic abilities.

Pregnancy and Enhanced Spirit Communication

Many people report enhanced advanced psychic abilities during pregnancy. The spirit of the child seems to come and go at will. It may speak to the person in dreams or appear in waking visions. The intelligence of this spirit seems to be perfectly formed, already displaying a distinct personality and an ability to give warnings and advice about future events.

This experience, also, applies to some miscarriages and stillbirths. After such an experience, the spirit of the child may continue to linger. A good palm reader can see all such parent-child relationships on the side of a person's hand, beneath the pinkie finger.

A powerful psychic connection appears to exist between many parents and their children. Parents often know, by means of telepathy or other advanced psychic ability, when their children are in danger and sometimes arrive just in the nick of time to prevent tragedy. It is sometimes called "mother's intuition" and, in its most advanced form, it can occur with very specific information obtained by clairvoyance, clairaudience, or claircognizance.

This natural connection between parents and children beyond the physical plane is often apparent even to people who do not generally regard themselves as psychics.

Trauma and Enhanced Psychic Abilities

Many people suddenly discover enhanced psychic abilities after severe trauma, which is an event or series of events that causes a person to feel that they are going to die. Survivors of domestic violence, kidnapping, sexual assault, and war, especially when these events are pro-longed, experience profound changes in their way of looking at the world, not only figuratively, but literally. According to conventional science, these experience cause measurable changes in the brain and are, in effect, a psychological injury that can be seen by brain imaging.

Surviving severe trauma seems to hack the matrix of common reality and causes people to wake up from the mass trance induced by the collective mindset. In effect, the person is forcibly detached from the common false reality, which includes such beliefs as "bad things only happen to bad people" and "the world is a relatively safe place."

Those who have survived severe trauma have experienced something unusual, something shocking, which has an impact on the way they perceive the world around them. This is why these experiences, especially very violent and tragic ones are like a kind of death. They cut the survivor off from the understanding of others. Those who experience such severe trauma have information about the world that they find difficult to share with others who are, effectively, still in a trance.

As a result of the trauma, survivors appear to develop more sophisticated internal warning systems, as a survival mechanism. They are able to see through and hear inside people's minds and, therefore, are better able to judge the probability of being in a dangerous situation than others because of enhanced clairaudient and clairvoyant abilities. Claircognizance is enhanced, too. Survivors of severe trauma are often able to know what is about to happen before it takes place. Often, this increases their sense of isolation because they have difficulty convincing others.

The relationship of severe trauma to advanced psychic abilities may be why many instances of precognition involve unpleasant events. It's these events about which we need to be warned. The good things that happen do not represent a danger to us, but the bad things do. Good people don't represent a danger, but bad people do.

Near Death Experiences

In some ways similar to severe trauma is the near death experience (N.D.E.), wherein a person is physically dead for a short period of time and then regains consciousness. This is a form of O.B.E., in which survivors see religious figures, angels, and deceased relatives. Classically, they report seeing a tunnel and being given the option to stay or return.

Very often, N.D.E.s activate advanced psychic abilities in survivors. One such case is that of Stella Horrocks, who experienced an N.D.E. in the hospital, after which she developed the ability to receive auditory communications from famous, deceased authors. Since that life-changing event, she has acted as the medium for hundreds of books and documents, which she believes were not the product of her own thoughts.[5]

Accounts of N.D.E.s often have strikingly similar characteristics. Various research organizations, such as the *International Association for Near Death Studies* (iands.org), have undertaken a study of these experiences.

A great number of survivors of N.D.E.s report, not only similar experiences during death, but increased psychic abilities afterward. Some researchers have theorized that the physical process of death may cause more of a naturally occurring substance called Dimethyltryptamine (D.M.T.) to be released in the pineal gland, which leads people to experience these strikingly similar "hallucinations" upon death.

Rick Strassman, who researched the relationship of N.D.E.s to D.M.T., concluded that this naturally occurring chemical plays a role in human spiritual experiences.[6] He wrote an important book on the subject, called *DMT: The Spirit Molecule: A Doctor's Revolutionary Research into the Biology of Near-Death and Mystical Experiences.*

The natural chemical D.M.T. is also found in other animals and plants, in particular, the amanita muscaria mushroom, salvia divinorum, and ayahuasca (Banisteriopsis caapi).

A shamanistic potion, called ayahuasca, combines the juice from the vines of this plant along with other D.M.T.-containing plants (typically, the leaves of psychotria viridis, psychotria carthaginensis, and diplopterys cabrerana, but there are many others), which are used to enhance and direct the experience. Shamans in Peru and Mexico use D.M.T.-containing plants to go into a trance state and communicate with spirits to obtain information about how to heal particular cases. Similar plants grow throughout the world and are quite possibly the foundation for the legends of witches' flying potions.

The late, great ethnomycologist, James Arthur, wrote a number of interesting theories based on his extensive research and experimentation with "magic mushrooms," in particular, the amanita muscaria and another class of mushrooms, called psilocybins. In his book, *Mushrooms and Mankind,* he concluded that these plants provide mankind with a doorway to other planes of reality.[7]

Arthur's research was preceded by the work of Dr. Robert Gordon Wasson, author of *Soma: Divine Mushroom of Immortality*; and Andrija Puharich, who was a mentor to Uri Gellar, a famous medical and parapsychological researcher, and the author of *The Sacred Mushroom: Key to the Door of Eternity.*

Despite the fact that D.M.T. is a naturally occurring substance in the human brain and in plants, it is a scheduled substance in the U.S. and many other countries.

Interestingly, the D.M.T. stored in the pineal gland is somewhat similar to serotonin (5-HT) and melatonin. The glandular system, of which the pineal gland is an important part, seems to provide a bridge between the physical body and its nervous system and the etheric, astral and mental bodies.

According to researchers, the brain chemical D.M.T. is not only released into the pineal gland upon death but, also, during R.E.M. sleep, which is the dream state. It is during this period of sleep that people report such phenomena as lucid dreams, prophetic communications, and astral projection. Perhaps a similar release of D.M.T. into the pineal gland occurs in cases of severe trauma among violent crime survivors, as well, which would account for their enhanced psychic abilities.

It is quite possible that hereditary psychics are born with higher amounts of this naturally occurring chemical in their pineal glands than other people. Certain life events, such as pregnancy, severe trauma, or N.D.E, may lead to fluctuations in D.M.T. and other naturally occurring bodily chemicals, which allow for certain types of advanced psychic experiences.

SOPHIA DIGREGORIO

Chapter 5
Detoxifying and Stimulating the Glandular and Nervous Systems

Presently, there is a broad assault on the glandular (endocrine) and nervous systems of the human body in the form of chemicals added to water, food, and other products. This assault is detrimental, not only to human health, but to the natural human ability to function on other planes of existence.

Sodium fluoride, a soft metal compound, is a by-product of the aluminum industry, which is purposely added to water supplies, most commercial toothpastes, and some mouthwashes. It bioaccumulates in the pineal gland and causes it to calcify, which is detrimental to the production of D.M.T.

Although its purveyors have tried to pass it off as such, sodium fluoride is not the naturally occurring trace mineral fluorine, which is required by the tissues of the body, especially bones and teeth. This toxic mimicker is, however, absorbed by the body whenever this beneficial trace mineral, fluorine, is deficient.

It is especially important for psychics to avoid fluoridated substances, although this is difficult because of the ubiquitous nature of this toxin in the food supply. Minimize your exposure by choosing distilled water over tap or drinking water, which has been found to contain not only fluoride but radioactive isotopes, pesticides, and other deadly chemicals. Choose more natural dentifrices over fluoridated ones.

Another approach to the problem of fluoride is to try to prevent the absorption of it into the tissues by supplementing the diet with natural sources of iodine, such as Sea-adine, Lugol's, and dulse kelp and other varieties of seaweed. These plants and plant derivatives, also, fight the effects of radiation, which have a detrimental effect on the entire glandular system and impair its ability to perform necessary secretions.

Chlorine is one of the most deadly substances known to mankind, yet it is added to tap water to "purify" it by government mandate. Chlorine literally suffocates living organisms. Furthermore, it is disruptive to the thyroid, which is the master gland of the glandular system.

Despite the assertions of marketing companies that sell chlorine products, it should never be used on food or in the house. Instead, choose healthier cleaning products. Diffuse essential oils like eucalyptus, peppermint, sage, and lavender to kill household bacteria and mold. Use homemade colloidal silver to disinfect produce and cleanse kitchen counter tops, bathrooms, and other areas prone to bacteria and mold growth.

Drinking and cooking with distilled water is a good way to avoid both fluoride and chlorine. But chemicals can be absorbed through the skin, too, during a bath or shower. Shower filters are a relatively inexpensive method of avoiding this problem.

The artificial flavor enhancer, MSG (Monosodium Glutamate), and artificial sweeteners, in particular, aspartame, are detrimental to the nervous system and should be avoided. MSG is present in many pre-prepared and restaurant foods.

Aspartame and other dangerous sweeteners are present in pre-prepared foods, sodas, and chewing gum. Raw sugar, raw honey, and coconut sugar are safer, more nutritional sweeteners.

Mercury is a heavy metal that disrupts the nervous system by disrupting neurotransmitters, which facilitate the communication of electric impulses within the body that allow thoughts, emotions, and voluntary motor functions to occur.

Mercury and mercury compounds are found in a great number of products, including some antiseptics and anti-fungal agents, tattoo inks, and some vaccines. It is associated with a broad range of neurological disorders, especially in children.

Gray or "silver" fillings are mercury amalgams that may slowly weaken and sicken a person, often without the victim understanding the cause of his or her thyroid imbalance, fatigue, hair loss, and headaches.

It is, also, found in mercury thermometers and the new economical mercury light bulbs. Thermometers do not pose a safety hazard unless they are broken. Mercury light bulbs are dangerous if broken and are said to continually emit mercury vapors into the environment whenever they are used.

Mercury can present a hazard to some workers and is present in the environment as a product of coal electricity production. It goes into the air, where it is breathed into the lungs, then it falls down into the water and soil where it enters the food and water supply.

High fructose corn syrup, a common sweetener used in processed foods and carbonated beverages, is a source of mercury.

Mercury can be present in toxic levels in sea fish. Because of bio-accumulation, levels are generally higher in larger fish. Therefore, it is recommended that swordfish, shark, and albacore tuna should be eaten sparingly, if at all. Lower-risk fish include catfish, crab, haddock, herring, pollock, trout, and wild salmon. Fish oil supplements may be highly beneficial, but do your own research on the source of the fish used in the production of the particular brand you choose because they are not well-regulated.

It is important to practice the avoidance of these toxins, as much as possible. Together with previous recommendations, whenever possible, choose organic food, which is not grown with the use of chemical pesticides.

How to Detoxify

One of the best and fastest ways to detoxify specific chemicals, like sodium fluoride, from the pineal gland is through radionics. Radionics might be described as a form of electronic homeopathy (although no batteries or conventional electricity is involved) using radio waves on a frequency just below the physical. It allows for the targeting of specific organs for specific toxins or conditions.

Although it is harmless, it is illegal to practice radionics on human beings (except one's self) in the United States, but it is part of some medical practices in other countries. In the U.S., it is practiced underground by individuals who are not medical doctors, but little is written about it because of the heavy suppression. The best information to date comes from the work of Bruce Copen of *Copen Labs* (www.copenlabs.com), who are, also, the manufacturers of highly regarded radionics equipment.

EDTA (Ethylene Diamine Tetra Acetic Acid) Chelation therapy is used in more dire cases of toxic contamination. It must be administered via I.V. by a qualified practitioner, however, in the U.S., such doctors and nurses are increasingly difficult to find. The *American College for Advancement in Medicine* (acam.org) certifies chelation therapists and may be able to provide a list of such people. This form of chelation detoxifies the body very quickly.

For most people, chelation can be sufficiently accomplished through nutrition, supplementation, and the application of naturally detoxifying substances. The purpose of all chelation is to unbind the toxins that are being held in the body and remove them. It is another term for detoxification of heavy metals.

Magnesium (Vitamin B-6) is important for broad-spectrum detoxification. Eat magnesium-rich foods such as barley grass, chocolate, nuts, dark green vegetables, dulse, kelp, nori, chlorella, and spirulina (blue-green algae).

Wheat grass is a highly nutritious food with many benefits, including heavy metal detoxification. Make it part of your daily diet. Organic wheat grass seeds are inexpensive and can be sprouted indoors. Wheat grass powder or fresh sprouts can be added to freshly made vegetable juice.

Detoxify mercury and other contaminants with bentonite clay. Dissolve one (1) tablespoon of bentonite clay in a glass of water with honey or in a glass of juice and consume it, at least, one hour before a meal or before falling asleep at night. After about a week, gradually, increase the amount of clay to four (4) tablespoons per day in divided doses. Do not take bentonite clay within an hour of consuming nutritious food, supplements, or important medication because it may absorb the benefits of these things.

Mercury can, also, be removed from the body by the daily intake of chlorella, wheat grass, and spirulina. Cilantro (coriander) herb taken daily can help remove mercury from brain tissue.

The important trace mineral boron is almost as important as iodine from dulse kelp in blocking the absorption of toxins by the glandular system. Experts recommend a supplement with 3 mg per day.

The homeopathic remedy, Borax in 30C potency, is a safe method of getting boron into the system.

Tamarind tea or tincture made from the bark, leaves, or pulp may help detoxify sodium fluoride from the pineal gland.

Detoxify with milk thistle supplements or tincture and raw juicing of carrots, beets, celery, and parsley.

Include a daily multivitamin supplement that supplies the necessary trace minerals. Selenium and chromium, in particular, are necessary for connecting with other planes of existence.

Detoxifying Baths:

Add two (2) cups of bentonite clay to two (2) cups of apple cider vinegar. Stir the mixture and add it to a hot bath. Soak for 20 to 30 minutes.

Alternatively, dissolve 1/4 cup of sea salt, one (1) tablespoon of baking soda, and 1/8 teaspoon boron (Borax cleaning powder) into a quart of water and add it to a hot bath. Soak for 20 to 30 minutes.

Add essential oils of sage, rosemary, or lavender to enhance the enjoyment of your bath, encourage further relaxation, and expand your vibratory range.

Naturally Increase D.M.T. Production

Although many D.M.T.-producing plants traditionally taken by shamans are scheduled substances, you can in crease your natural production with the right diet and sleep practices.

The following suggestions are relatively safe, however, it is suggested that you check with your doctor before taking any supplements or herbs, especially if you are pregnant, nursing, under the care of a physician, or taking anti-depressants or other drugs as some herbs can interfere with them.

Natural D.M.T. production in the pineal gland is facilitated by melatonin production. The following melatonin-producing foods and herbs will help you to have more powerful dreams, which is a sign that you are psychic abilities are increasing. You may consume the following throughout the day, however, taking one or two of them before bedtime will yield the best results.

Add 1/2 tablespoon dried, powdered ginger or several thin slices of the fresh root to approximately one cup of boiling water to make a tea. Sweeten it, if you like. Ginger is a natural, melatonin-producing sleep aid.

A serving of acai berry juice taken before bedtime may produce very vivid, colorful dreams. All dark-colored berries and their fresh juices help the pineal gland to produce the precursory chemicals to D.M.T. production.

Melatonin is produced naturally when you consume foods that contain tryptophan such as turkey, spirulina, cod fish, and seeds of pumpkin, sesame, and sunflower. Egg whites are a very good source of melatonin, but take caution with them if you live in the U.S.

U.S. chickens have been given feed laced with pharmaceutical antibiotics containing arsenic or some other potentially harmful chemical. Consuming eggs or chicken can produce noticeable health problems especially in girls and women, which manifest as severe abdominal pain and profuse hemorrhaging during menses. If you live in the U.S., consume eggs, egg-containing products, or chicken and are experiencing these symptoms, experiment with eliminating both eggs and chicken from your diet for a month or so to see if the condition improves. Eggs from chickens not given this feed should be safe and beneficial to eat because both the yolk and white contain melatonin, although the white contains a far higher amount.

For those suffering from anxiety, mild muscular pain, or insomnia, a combination of valerian root and lemongrass is a highly effective, deeply relaxing remedy. Both herbs are powerful as a tea or tincture, but especially as a decoction.

Place a dried valerian root approximately 1" in length or 1/2 tablespoon crushed valerian root and 1/2 tablespoon dried lemongrass into a pan of approximately two (2) cups of distilled water. Allow the herbs to boil in the water for 3 to 5 minutes. Remove it from the heat and allow it to cool. Strain the liquid into a cup and consume it immediately before retiring. This remedy is even more powerful if you repeat it, again, the following day.

Natural D.M.T. production is aided by darkness. Therefore, before you lie down to sleep, take care to shut out all outside light sources. It is ideal to have black-out shades on your windows and heavy curtains you can pull to block out the light. If necessary, pin or tape the curtains or put a blanket over the window, if you must, to block out all of the light and create a completely dark room. If this is not entirely possible, use a sleeping mask or gently tie a scarf around your eyes so you cannot perceive any light while you sleep.

Further deepen your sleep by eliminating disruptive sounds. Some people sleep better with the sound of a fan or the white noise created by a radio set off a station. Some devices, called "white noise machines," are designed for this purpose and produce not only white noise, but other soothing sounds for sleep that help to block out interfering noise from outside sources.

Another option is to sleep with ear plugs. Some people find them uncomfortable, but if they do not bother you, you will sleep far more deeply with them. Furthermore, wearing ear plugs at night seems to increase auditory sensitivity when they are not being worn.

Abbreviation Key for Measurements

T. = tablespoon
tsp. = teaspoon
oz. = ounce
g = gram
mg = milligrams

Conversion of Measurements

3 tsp. = 1 T.
1 tsp. = approximately 4.2 g
1 cup liquid = approximately 220 to 240 g
1 cup non-liquid = approximately 120 to 140 g
1 g = 1000 mg
1 mg = 0.001 grams

Chapter 6
The Psychic Diet

Not only does a healthy diet of natural, unprocessed foods help clean up heavy metals and neurotoxins, thus, improving the function of the glandular system and even reversing some dire cases of nerve poisoning, it has special benefits to people who are interested in increasing their psychic abilities.

Vegetarianism has been a practice of occultists for centuries. In fact, it is sometimes the hallmark of a serious occultist. But it isn't necessarily a religious practice, as some people might think. Consuming raw fruits and vegetables and their juices, which contain a supply of essential life force, increases your own life force energy and increases your vibratory rate, enlarging your range of sensory perception outside of the common, physical plane.

Vegetarianism is not for everyone and it is not necessarily healthy for everyone. But the practice need not be radical or long-term for positive effects on the enhancement of extra-sensory perception to be achieved. In fact, a semi-vegetarian diet that includes fish can be especially powerful.

One of the best ways to get a large amount of living nutrients into your body is through juicing. Start slow with raw vegetable juicing because, if you are very toxic, it can cause nausea. Slowly increase the daily amount from 1/2 cup to one (1) cup per day to, at least, a quart of juice from fresh carrots, beets, celery, parsley, and wheat grass sprouts per day.

Carrots help to "lighten" the physical body and seem to do the most to raise the vibrational frequencies. Celery increases the ability to be calm and focused. Beets are detoxifying and impart powerful energy. Parsley and wheat grass are highly nutritious nerve tonics. To chelate heavy metals like mercury, include a handful of fresh cilantro into your daily regimen.

ORME (Orbitally Rearranged Monotomic Elements or "m-state elements") is the name for a controversial substance that is sometimes sold online as a supplement. It is credited with rapid, advanced psychic development. The process for the creation of ORME was patented by David Hudson, a cotton farmer from Phoenix, Arizona, who first discovered this curious substance in his soil and had it analyzed by a laboratory. Some people believe this substance is the original, white powder of gold of the alchemists. Many people report a pronounced increase in clairaudient and clairvoyant abilities from ingesting very small amounts of ORME.

ORME is sometimes called "ORMUS." There are various procedures available on the Internet for extracting ORME or ORMUS from sea salt, although there is no data and little anecdotal evidence for the efficacy of these processes, their outcomes or, the safety of the substance they may produce.

Rhodium and iridium are two important trace minerals that are in ORME.[8] Both can be obtained from natural sources, are highly beneficial to your overall health, and produce an increase in the body's vibratory rate. Rhodium is present in high concentration in carrots, while iridium is present in Essiac Tea (a four-herb combination sold as Guardian Spirit Tea by Frontier Coop, in the U.S.). The four herbs in this tea, which has an excellent reputation for fighting cancer, are burdock root, sheep sorrel, slippery elm, and Turkey rhubarb. This herbal combination can be taken as a tea, in capsule form, or as a tincture. For more information about Essiac, visit www.essiacinfo.org.

If you juice and include the above foods in your vegetarian or semi-vegetarian regimen for several weeks, you may notice an improvement in your physical vision as well as your psychic abilities. Physical sight and etheric sight are closely related and both rely heavily on the proper functioning of the nervous system.

Essential fatty acids are important to brain function and help fight some mental disorders such as depression. Ground flax seed, flax seed oil, and chia seeds are very good plants sources. Chia seeds are packed with nutrition and very helpful for people who aren't sure they're getting enough nutrients in their diets.

Certain otherwise innocuous and even beneficial foods should be avoided because they interfere with psychic ability. During your active attempts to expand your advanced psychic abilities, avoid red meat, nuts, and other heavy foods, which lower the vibratory rate and decrease the vibratory range.

Vegetarianism can open up advanced psychic abilities in a very stark way, which is why consuming the aforementioned foods, particularly beef, can be used as a helpful mechanism for temporarily turning them off, if they begin to become overwhelming to the psychic. The effects last for approximately one to three days.

To improve your overall health and psychic abilities, combine the practice of vegetarianism with meditation, wherein the goal is to clear the mind or focus on a particular object. Such exercises are suggested below.

The Importance of Avoiding Toxic Drugs and Over-Consumption of Alcohol

All toxic drugs should be avoided by practicing or developing psychics, however, the most detrimental among pharmaceuticals is the class of drugs known as SSRIs (Selective Serotonin Reuptake Inhibitors), which are typically used in the treatment of depression, anxiety, and some types of personality disorders.

These drugs, which are more commonly known by brand names such as Paxil, Prozac, Luvox, and Zoloft among others, interfere with the function of the neurotransmitter serotonin. Both melatonin and serotonin are naturally manufactured by the body in the pineal gland and are precursors to D.M.T. production.

These prescription drugs are, at least, as dangerous as illicit drugs like Crystal Meth (methamphetamines). All of them cause delusions, and people have been known to commit all kinds of violent acts upon themselves and others while under their influence. The use of SSRI's is frequently a footnote to acts of mass violence reported in the news, including school and other mass shootings.

Generally speaking, any drug initially created in a government or pharmaceutical laboratory, such as methamphetamines, L.S.D., or cocaine in its numerous forms, is dangerous to psychics and detrimental to psychic development.

One of the worst among these, methamphetamine or Crystal Meth, has gained popularity to the point of being epidemic in some parts of the U.S. The psychological profile of a methamphetamine user is that of a demon. Under the influence of this drug, users commit many extremely perverse and violent crimes because, while this drug does expand the ability to see and hear on non-physical vibratory frequency ranges, it, also, pokes holes in the natural defenses, thereby making the user vulnerable to possession by dark entities.

Just like toxic drugs, alcohol consumption should be avoided before and during any practices intended to increase psychic abilities, such as divination or communicating with spirits.

Consuming alcohol dulls the senses, which is counterproductive to psychic development. Furthermore, alcohol consumption weakens the natural defenses and opens up the drinker to the possibility of obsession, possession, or psychic attack. The importance of avoiding alcohol is well-known to those who traverse the "left-hand path," because a part of this practice involves the domination of dark entities.

Therefore, the consumption of both toxic drugs and alcohol is commonly avoided by many serious occultists.

Chapter 7
Meditation Techniques for Advanced Psychic Development

Meditation is fundamental to developing advanced psychic abilities. Unfortunately, it is not the most exciting exercise. But it is a powerful one, especially when it is practiced daily even for short periods of time.

There are different types of meditation, but each essentially has the same purpose, which is to discipline the mind, increase its power and sustain its ability to be both relaxed and focused. It is in this state of relaxed focus that you are able to tune your mind, similar to how you would tune a radio, to different frequencies.

Life for most Westerners is full of artificial stresses of all kinds. Therefore, it is more difficult to find the time to meditate or engage in any kind of relaxing activities. But you must try because even in trying you will make some progress. Furthermore, a relaxed state of focus with greater control over your mind is beneficial not only to psychic development, but vital to overall health.

It is necessary to be in a quiet, relaxing environment where you feel safe. It is nearly impossible to begin or maintain a healthy practice of meditation in an environment where there is a lot of drama of any kind.

A dark environment with lights turned down helps induce a meditative state. Darkness stimulates the pineal gland and increases its production of D.M.T., which facilitates easier achievement of the trance state.

For people who have difficulty escaping disruptive family members and other household pressures, the bathroom is the only place they can expect privacy. Regardless, it is actually a very good practice to set aside a few minutes of your soak in the bathtub to meditate.

Take beads, a candle, a crystal and whatever else you plan to use with you. Light a candle and turn out the light so you are in near darkness. Close your eyes and conduct a simple breathing meditation.

Plan to do the following exercise of 15 breathing repetitions given below.

Before you begin, you may find it helpful to pass all of your foremost thoughts and concerns through your mind and dismiss them one by one. As the unwanted thought comes into your mind, dismiss it by saying, "I will think about you more later." Western culture is very work-oriented, so it may help to tell yourself that this meditation is your job and it is what you are supposed to be doing for the next few minutes. This is a way of giving your subconscious mind permission to relax.

During the course of your meditation, if a thought other than that of your breath going in and out comes into your head, simply dismiss it. Do not berate yourself for it. Just go back to focusing on the breath.

The simple exercise is as follows: Inhale for the count of 6, and hold it for a count of 2; exhale for a count of 6, and hold for a count of 2. Repeat.

Begin by doing 15 repetitions. Afterward, rest and then, if you feel like doing it, again, you may.

Maintain your focus on the act of breathing and nothing else. As you do so, see healthy vital energy going into the body upon each inhale and depleted, dirty energy being released upon exhale.

This is more easily done with some meditation beads or a rosary, so you can take your mind off the act of counting and simply move your fingers on the beads and focus on breathing.

Even if the only time per day you do this is in the bath, this simple exercise will improve your ability to relax and focus. By practicing this little bit of control over your mind, you will have an easier time quieting your mind and getting your mental chatter under control at will.

The more you do it, the easier it becomes and the more you recognize the benefits.

As you become more proficient with your meditation and if it suits you to do so, look further into the Eastern practice of yoga. It isn't for everybody, but it may be for you.

Hatha yoga, which is the yoga of breath is generally the most easily embraced by Westerners. In *Book 4*, the accomplished occultist Aleister Crowley instructs the reader in yogic meditation, providing an excellent description of the practice, the postures and the use of mantras. He, also, addresses both the difficulties and the benefits of the practice. His approach is naturally Westernized and easily adaptable to modern life.

There are many other ways to meditate. In fact, meditation is similar to some forms of prayer. Depending on your particular belief or temperament, you might find the recitation of the Rosary or favorite Psalms highly beneficial. Below are two other possibilities.

An Old Latin Benedictine Exorcism Prayer:

*Vade retro Satana! Numquam suade mihi vana! Sunt mala quae libas. Ipse venena biba*s!

Translation: *Begone Satan! Never tempt me with your vanities! What you offer me is evil. Drink the poison yourself!*

Obstacle Breaking Sanskrit Mantra to Lord Ganesha:

Om gam ganapataye namaha!

Pronounced evenly, as follows: *Aum-gam-gana-pata-yea-na-ma-hah!*

Deepen your trance by taking two energizing breath repetitions of 6-2-6-2, as given above before beginning. Classically, Sanskrit mantras are repeated 108 times in reverent, focused meditation, however, the above mantra can bring a sense of relaxation and mastery of yourself and your environment in just a few repetitions. There is power in the sound of the syllables, particularly, in ancient languages like Sanskrit and Latin, which is why the syllables are sung.

Drumming is another very powerful form of inducing meditation. Like every other method, it works better for some people than others. So, you should experiment with this to find out if it is a good way for you to achieve a focused, meditative state.

In the U.S. the practice of drumming is associated with the ancient shamanic practices of the American Indians. Done correctly, it is said to mimic the frequencies within the planet, itself and it helps those who hear it to achieve harmonic resonance with nature. It is often used by groups of people and can be combined with prayer or guided meditation. You may find that listening to recordings of Indian drumming helps you achieve a relaxed meditative state.

Practicing meditation regularly helps a person reach a trance state more quickly and maintain it, even when there are outside distractions. This ability is helpful in all other endeavors.

Anchoring is a technique used by hypnotists. You can easily use this technique to condition your mind to go into a relaxed, focused state upon certain cues. These may be a certain hand position, glancing at a certain color, taking a certain number of breaths or some other short ritual that signals your mind to go into this altered state. This is something you can incorporate into your practice of meditation.

For example, tell yourself when you take two deep breaths, close your eyes and visualize the color black, your mind will automatically go into a trance state. Incorporate this into whatever other meditation practice you choose as a preliminary procedure. If you do this regularly, you will find that these signals will allow you to go into a trance nearly at will.

In our fast-paced and often frenzied modern culture, multi-tasking is valued. People brag about their ability to eat breakfast, drive the kids to school and arrange appointments all at the same time. It is even listed as a positive asset of prospective employees on their resumes. But, if you want to develop your advanced psychic abilities, you must resist this popular trend and discipline your mind to focus on only one thing at a time. This begins as a conscious mental shift. You must accept that the ability to focus intently on the task at hand is a virtue and a valuable skill.

Then, apply focused concentration to as many tasks as you can. For example, when you read a book, think of nothing else until you have finished it. If your mind begins to wander, make it stop. To do this, address your mind as if it were a misbehaving child. Say to it, "Now, mind, you must focus on what you are doing here and nothing else for a short time. When you are finished with this task, you will be free to wander, again."

If you are gardening, knitting, painting a picture or engaging in any task whatsoever, focus your mind on just that one effort. Do this for short periods of time and soon you will be able to do it for longer periods of time. The ability to focus your mind in this way is a valuable skill that you can develop quickly with a little effort.

The Detrimental Effects of Television

There is a very common frequency altering device that may be having a detrimental effect on your ability to focus and perceive the fullness of your sensory range. This potential obstacle to psychic development is your television.

Numerous studies have been conducted over the past several decades exploring the hypnotic effect of television on the mind. Although it is only necessary to observe someone who is watching television to see the effect it has on them. They are lethargic and seem to be half asleep as they become passive receptors to whatever images and messages are being broadcast on the screen.

If you don't watch television, you may have noticed that people who do are difficult to communicate with. Watching television reduces their ability to focus and concentrate. Their minds adapt to the rhythm of television programming, flitting from one idea to the next, often illogically.

Furthermore, television creates many false perceptions about the world, so that people who watch it very much seem to live in a collective reality separate from those who do not. It is literally programming people's minds to a false reality and altering their brainwave patterns, even when they are not engaged in television watching at the time.

A lot of what is broadcast on the television seems to be designed to upset people emotionally, as well. It is not conducive to a calm, meditative, and focused mental state. For these reasons, it is advisable to reduce the amount of television you watch or eliminate the habit entirely as you try to advance your psychic abilities.

Chapter 8
Herbs, Crystals, and Potions

The following herbs and crystals can be used to facilitate psychic abilities and enhance the quality of dreams and visions:

Use a tea or tincture of clary sage, elecampane, eyebright, or sage for increased psychic abilities.

Make a tea of red rose petals or dissolve 1/2 oz. of rosehip powder in distilled water for the health of the heart and to raise your vibrational frequency to higher planes.

Stop mental chatter with a tea of star anise.

Drink a tea made of dried thyme to facilitate resonance with the frequencies of the akashic records.

Brew a tea with a pinch each of thyme, rose, and anise, and drink it before any psychic endeavor.

Place a sachet of mugwort, vervain, and lavender under your pillow to facilitate astral dreaming.

Mugwort may be used as a tea or tincture, but can have a strong estrogenic effect, so take caution. Do not use it daily. Do not take mugwort internally during pregnancy.

Inhale strong peppermint oil to clear the sinuses and breathe more freely for meditation and to open up psychic awareness.

Apply sandalwood essential oil to the third eye to increase psychic abilities.

Add dragon's blood resin oil to other anointing preparations and use it to anoint a cloth, medicine bag, or stones you are using for meditation. It imparts fiery energy and powerful protection, especially against dark, lower astral energies.

Meditate with an apophyllite crystal in hand or nearby for help contacting other planes and the akashic records for information from the past, present, or future.

Meditate with moldavite in hand or nearby to contact extra-terrestrial entities and gain knowledge about other worlds.

Sleep with a long selenite wand under your bed to automatically align the chakras.

Keep three different shades of tiger's eye (red, yellow and blue) with you in a pouch (mojo bag). Occasionally, anoint the stones with sandalwood oil. Also, hold the stones in your hands during meditation to help open up the third eye.

The following formulas are from the book, *Traditional Witches' Formulary and Potion-making Guide: Recipes for Magical Oils, Powders and Other Potions,* by Sophia diGregorio:

Psychic Powder
(Increase psychic abilities)

Increases psychic powers and produces prophetic dreams. Sprinkle on bed sheets, tarot cards, or rune stones, or dust some on yourself. Recipe is for 6-10 uses.

1/2 oz. Orris Root powder
2 tsp. Vetivert
1 tsp. Amber resin
1 tsp. Mugwort
1 tsp. Chicory

Psychic Visions Incense

2 T. Gum mastic
2 T. Juniper
1 T. Cinnamon
1 T. Calamus
A pinch of Amber resin
A pinch of Patchouli

Talisman for Psychic Visions

Fill a mojo bag with any of the following herbs and keep it with you: Acacia twigs, Anise, Caraway, Dandelion root, Mace, Mugwort, Rose, Saffron, Sumbul, Thyme, or Uva Ursi.

Spell for Psychic Development

The most beneficial times to do a spell for psychic development are during the dark of the moon (or new moon) and waxing moon; when the moon is in the sign of Scorpio or Sagittarius; or on Thursday, which is the day of Jupiter.

Doing a simple spell or meditation to enhance your psychic ability can help signal your subconscious mind that you are ready to receive new information. It may, also, be used to send a signal out into the universe that you are ready to expand your psychic powers.

The following is a simple but effective meditation spell: Obtain a blue candle. Anoint it with essential oils of cinnamon, patchouli, and amber, using a motion toward you as if you are drawing these energies toward you.

Repeat the words, "Bring psychic powers to me; let it be, let it be."

Place the candle on a safe, sturdy table or prepared altar. You may scatter Psychic Powder or some of the dried herbs from the other formulas above around the candle.

Then, light the candle, dim the lights, and focus your meditation on the flame of the candle while repeating the above incantation with feeling. As you do, visualize your physical body's energy field increasing. Allow yourself to feel a flow of powerful energy coming into your body from all directions, expanding your awareness.

You may, also, appeal to any deity, angel, saint, or other helpful entity to help you enhance this ability.

Chapter 9
Tools and Methods for Advanced Psychic Development

Together with attention to diet and the practice of meditation, there are numerous tools and methods that can be employed to help train your mind and render it more accustomed to receiving information through clairvoyance and clairaudience.

Using divination tools can permanently open up your psychic abilities, especially if you really acquire an enthusiasm for using them. Becoming skillful at divination or some form of spirit communication increases your confidence and provides proof positive of psychic phenomena, thereby destroying any subconscious blockages you may have.

Dedication to the study of palm reading (cheiromancy), rune reading, the Kabbalah, the I Ching, tea leaf reading, astrology, or tarot cards inevitably leads to broader and more sophisticated psychic abilities.

Initially, these abilities increase only during the act of divination, but after the study and practice is continued for a long period of time, the psychic comes to a point where he or she can receive information with or without them.

One of the most powerful methods for opening up advanced psychic abilities is the in-depth study and application of tarot reading. Once you have mastered the basics of card reading and gotten used to handling the cards, do not continue to rely on tarot manuals. Instead, incorporate a study of the Kabbalah with astrology to penetrate deeper into the symbolism of the cards. Doing this broadens your abilities with the cards very quickly and takes you from being an adequate reader to an amazing one.

Becoming adept with the tarot and regularly using them to read for people you've never met, will open up your abilities far beyond using the cards themselves, which are no mere prop, as the uninitiated commonly assert. This expansion of psychic abilities and how it unfolds itself through the study and practice of the tarot reading is discussed in the treatise, *How to Read the Tarot for Fun, Profit and Psychic Development,* by Angela Kaelin.

Similarly, becoming proficient at palm reading can expand your advanced psychic abilities very quickly. Palmistry is a very nearly exact science as it was given by the old masters, whose very detailed books on the subject are most reliable.

Studying this subject and practicing your skills on strangers who give you honest feedback is another way to develop powerful psychic abilities. The following two books are among the very best for the serious student:

Cheiro, *Palmistry for All,* G.P. Putnam's Sons, 1916. (www.gutenberg.org)

Saint-Germain, C. de, *Practice of Palmistry,* Newcastle Publishing Company, 1973.

Ouija Boards and Automatic Writing

Advanced psychic abilities often develop out of dedicated experimentation with Ouija boards and similar tools.

While Ouija boards are often superstitiously shunned by the pop culture-addled public, especially in the U.S., they are a valuable mediumship-development tool and should never be feared by those who are making a serious inquiry into what lies beyond the ordinary range of the physical senses.

Just as with mediumship development circles, Ouija boards work best when they are used on a regular schedule. One or two operators can use the board at a time. The benefit to having a second person is the additional etheric energy that is brought to the situation. But one person can operate a board effectively with practice.

The Ouija board is, also, a beneficial meditation tool because it provides an object for relaxed focus.

The practice of automatic writing is similar to that of using a Ouija board. But it is a very simple and usually a solitary practice that involves sitting quietly with a pen and paper and giving a spirit permission to use your hand to write out messages.

This process begins slowly at first, but then becomes easier. As you progress, you learn to separate your own thoughts from those that come from an outside source. Eventually, you begin to receive very explicit messages, answers to questions you pose, and vivid imagery that supplies detailed information.

Crystal Balls

Crystal balls are beautiful, but they, too, are more than just props. Used properly, they can help you to develop your clairvoyance and clairaudience.

There are two main types of quartz crystal balls used for scrying: Natural and reconstituted. The methods for using either of these vary only slightly.

The easiest to read are those carved and polished from a natural piece of quartz crystal, which has all of the fissures, inclusions, and rainbow-like sparkles in it.

Theoretically, you can read a crystal of any size, however, larger crystals have a greater supply of natural energy, which can help you to keep your focus and magnify your abilities. Therefore, choose a natural crystal ball that is, at least, 3" in diameter.

Quartz crystal collects, retains, and radiates whatever energetic impressions have been placed into it either intentionally or unintentionally. Therefore, you should clear your crystal before you use it, especially if you have just acquired it.

There are different methods for cleansing a crystal, such as holding it under running water, placing it in a dish of sea salt, or allowing it to sit in the sunlight. A quick and effective method is to simply pass your hand over the crystal a few times as a mesmerist would while mentally commanding it to clear.

Place your natural crystal ball on a small stand and find a comfortable place to sit where you can focus your attention on the ball. Then, darken the room except for one candle, which should be placed about 3 to 4' away from the ball, either off to one side or a little bit behind you as you are sitting at the table.

Take a couple of deep breaths and tell yourself to relax. You are now going to read the crystal ball. You will focus on this task and nothing else for the next several minutes. Tell yourself that it is your job to do this, so that your subconscious mind has permission to relax and focus.

Formulate a question in your mind to which you would like to have an answer. If it is applicable, frame your question in terms of a definite time period, such as one month from now, six months from now, and so on.

Look into the crystal ball and take note of any recognizable images or symbols you see. Turn the crystal slightly this way and that until you see an image that strikes you as significant. Notice what other feelings, sensations, visions, sounds, or any other impressions come into your mind in association with the image.

If you are working with an audio recorder or another person, describe aloud what you see and your impressions surrounding it. If you are working alone without a recorder, write this information down. After your session is over, you may continue to receive more information about what you have seen and you will have your notes for reference.

If you are doing readings for other people, you may want to devise a system. For example, conduct your reading on the basis of three images that you see in the crystal ball. Assign them to the past, present, and future, in that order.

The second type of crystal ball is the completely clear, reconstituted quartz variety. These balls are usually much larger than the all-natural ones and very visually striking. They are generally far less expensive than all-natural crystal balls, but the biggest advantage is the greater kinetic energy they possess. The energy of a reconstituted crystal is much more intense.

Larger, heavier crystal balls are best placed on a black pillow filled with sand or grain. As mentioned previously, darken the room, light a candle and place it nearby and maybe even slightly at an angle behind you. Clear the crystal and put yourself into a trance.

Formulate your question and look into the crystal ball. You will not see images based on any fissures or imperfections within the crystal because there are none. What you will see is a reflection of your inner mind.

Place your hands, with fingers outspread, about an inch or so away from the ball without touching it and project your question into the ball. Feel the heat radiating from the palms of your hands and your fingers as you do so. When you feel you have focused on this sufficiently, relax and assume a passive mental state.

Gaze into the ball and wait patiently. Usually in a matter of minutes, you will begin to see something, even if it is not fully formed. You may only see clouds or symbols at first. As you go on staring at the ball, more definite impressions will come into your mind in the form of pictures and sounds. You may see scenes, faces, places, and even scenarios, which may be accompanied by sounds and emotion.

Do not try to edit or deny what you are seeing or hearing during this process. Just let it happen. After the vision is complete and all of the information is received, record it in some way. Then, you can begin to analyze it from a more logical standpoint.

In the beginning, you may want to use the correlations between symbols and their meanings from dream books and tea leaf reading manuals as a guide. But the most important thing is to ask yourself what the visions and sounds you experience mean to you. This is a very individual thing. It does not remain fixed and may vary from reading to reading.

Scrying Mirrors

Scrying mirrors, which are mirrors made of black glass or carved from onyx, are another good alternative. These can be used without darkening the room as much. You place your focus on the surface of the mirror and proceed very much as you would when reading a reconstituted crystal ball.

The mirror serves not only as a focal point, but can help train your mind to go into a trance state very quickly. This skill can be applied to other techniques for advanced psychic development, rendering the mirror less necessary over time.

Learn to Do Energy Healing

Learning to do energy healing helps increase your sensitivity and expands your sensory awareness. There are many different methods of energy healing that involve the use of the mind to manipulate the chakra centers (the astral bridge to the glandular system), the etheric, and physical bodies.

The basics of this kind of psychic healing are given in the book, *Magical Healing: How to Use Your Mind to Heal Yourself and Others,* by Angela Kaelin. You can use these systems, especially *Magical Healing,* to heal yourself and others by seeing and manipulating the body on the etheric and astral planes. Those unfamiliar with such methods of healing will be amazed at how fast and efficient they are, especially in acute cases.

Reiki is a very popular system developed in 1922 by a Buddhist named Mikao Usui and popularized in the U.S. by Diane Stein with her series of books on the subject, beginning with *Essential Reiki: A Complete Guide to an Ancient Healing Art.* It is worth becoming familiar with, although it is limiting and dogmatic compared to similar systems.

A very precise form of energy healing is described in a series of books by Choa Kok Sui, called *Pranic Healing.* In these books he gives very specific energetic healing prescriptions for a wide variety of physical ailments.

Another excellent system based on the polarity of the body's energetic flow is given by Donna Eden in *The Energy Medicine Kit,* which includes a book and DVD that show you how to heal numerous conditions by what might be called "the laying on of hands."

Acupressure and reflexology help you to learn about the body's flow of life energy along the meridians. Learning these methods of healing help you to awaken and become more conscious of your latent psychic abilities.

These systems all help you to understand the nature of the energetic fields that surround and flow through the human body, which gives you a foundation on which to further expand your abilities and explain your experiences to yourself and others.

If you choose to work with other people in a group, as Reiki healers often do, you will have the opportunity to share your experiences and get feedback from supportive people. This is very helpful, especially early in your development when you are still wondering if what you are experiencing is real.

If you work with any of these systems, please remember this: No one can give you the power of healing, or for that matter clairvoyance, clairaudience, or claircognizance, because you already have that power. And, more than anyone else, you have the ability to use it. You don't need anyone else to confer it on you.

Reading the Astral (Emotional) Body

The concept of thought forms was developed and best described by Annie Besant and C.W. Leadbeater in their book, *Thought Forms*. With its color plates, the book provides a very good artistic depiction of the energies that can be seen by clairvoyants, which seem to exist on the less dense astral plane. This book is decades old, but it is still the best place to derive an understanding of this aspect of clairvoyance.

When conditions are just right and a person is standing, at least, a couple of feet away from you in front of a solid, light-colored background, you may see brightly colored lights radiating from the person's body.

The light has the color and the iridescent quality of the rainbow or the prism of colors that you see when you look through a clear quartz crystal. These are often pastel colors of pink, yellow, green, blue, and lavender, which are the colors you will see radiating from a person with a healthy mind and body. These emanations provide specific information about the person's mental and emotional state.

During intellectual discourse, if you move your eyes to the side of a person's head, you may see a vibrant yellow color radiating from it. A mother holding a child may have the color pink between them. The head of a religious devotee in prayer may be surrounded by blue. Lavender indicates the mindset of selfless giving, while shades of red show passion in the form of anger or sensuality.[9]

Usually, you will see a combination of colors that do not remain steady, but emerge and merge into others.

While the guide to the meaning of the colors given by Besant and Leadbeater seems to be mostly correct, you will have to use your own judgment as to the meaning of some of them. No one seems to have it down to an exact science.

For instance, there are different meanings to the gray color you see around people. It can mean fear or it can be an indicator that the person's life force is weak.

A very dark gray or black shadow around a person can indicate imminent death. But as previously mentioned, it can be an indicator of malice and pure evil, also. This is something you will have to assess case by case.

Animals, flowers, plants, and all other living things produce a radiant field. Keep this in mind throughout your day and look for opportunities to see these fields. External conditions have to be right. You will see them spontaneously, often when you least expect it.

Reading the Mental Body

This manifestation of colors on the astral plane is preceded by action on the mental plane. While reading the astral body gives you a lot of information, being able to intercept the thoughts of a person gives you even more.

With some relaxed concentration, it is possible to see and hear what is at the fore of a person's mind. The inner monologue or the dominant thoughts that people play and re-play in their minds can be tapped into just like any other frequency. This activity takes place on the level of the mental frequencies or the mental body and it yields very specific information in the form of images and words.

Skilled psychics are able to draw the mental energy from another person to themselves and, thereby, receive specific information about them. This can include all kinds of details, such as where they grew up, where they've been and significant things they have done.

Sometimes this happens during tarot readings or other types of divination. You will feel that you are pulling an energy field from the other person's mind toward your own.

This is something you could practice with a friend where you take turns sitting quietly trying to read a particular image or thought that they are holding in the fore of their mind for the purpose of the experiment.

But another way to develop this skill is to keep it in mind throughout your day as you come in contact with people. Don't tell them what you're doing. Doing so will either make them nervous or they'll think something is wrong with you. But be aware that the people around you have mental fields that you can draw toward you. Practice visualizing that field around their minds and pulling it toward your own.

You have an excellent opportunity to read a person's mind when you are introduced to them. Shake the person's hand and look into their eyes as you greet them and allow yourself to mentally penetrate the concentrated mental field centered on the pineal gland just behind the forehead.

The act of making physical contact while looking into the person's eyes creates a very powerful psychic connection through which you may receive vivid images. These may appear in your mind similar to a memory of your own projected onto a mental screen.

After you have succeeded at reading people's minds at will, you will find that it begins to happen more often spontaneously. Sometimes you will have strange thoughts or images in your mind that aren't your own and you don't know where they came from. Often these are the things at the fore of someone's mind and, if you let them converse with you without interruption, they will start talking about those exact things. This is your confirmation that you are tapping into their mental energy field.

In general, it seems that more sophisticated minds yield more sophisticated imagery and information to the psychic. People who are of a more base, emotional nature really do have less sophisticated mental activity. It is much easier to read an intelligent person's mind than it is to read the mind of a dullard.

Dowsing

Dowsing is a method of using a hand-held device to intercept and interpret frequencies outside the ordinary range of perception. Typically, a dowser uses a pendulum, rods, a twig, or a singular device, called a bobber, to find water, minerals, hidden treasure, lost objects, and missing people.

The application of the pendulum to gain information is a very simple one and you can devise all kinds of systems of your own for determining answers, based on the binary response of "Yes" or "No."

There are spiral-bound books that are nothing but pendulum charts for various purposes, but you can easily draw up your own. Alternatively, people use the letters from the Scrabble board or a Ouija board to ask more complex questions. Commonly, maps are employed, and a pendulum is used to find minerals and potable water sources hidden beneath the earth's surface. When dowsing is done on location, it is more common to use a twig, dowsing rods, or a bobber.

You may begin your dowsing experiments using a pendulum, which is a small weight suspended from a string or chain. Any small weight, such as a ring suspended from a piece of string, will do temporarily, however, every serious dowser should have a pendulum that is balanced and comfortable to hold. Most metaphysical stores sell such devices.

There are different ways to program a pendulum. You can hold it out in front of you and command it to show you the movements that mean "Yes" and "No" for you. Or, you can tell it which movement to make for these responses. For example, it is common for an up and down motion to mean "Yes," while a side to side motion means "No." Although some people prefer to use circular motions, where a clockwise motion means "Yes," and a counter-clockwise motion means "No."

Test your pendulum by asking it questions to which you already know the answer. For example, "Is my name _____?" "Is today Wednesday?"

After you have established the signals your pendulum will give you and tested them, you may begin using and devising new systems to help increase your clairvoyance.

For example, use your pendulum to determine the winning numbers in the lottery. Choose a simple lottery game that ask for three to five numbers.

There are many different ways you can use the pendulum to determine the winning numbers for the next lottery drawing.

One method is to create a chart or list of every possible winning number. Then, hold the pendulum over the number and ask if this is the winning number for that drawing on that date.

Sometimes people develop a bias for or against a particular number. If you feel this is occurring, try a method in which the numbers are hidden from your physical sight. Write each possible winning number on a 1" x 1" square of colored or heavy paper. Then place the pieces upside down and shuffle them. Afterward, use the same method with the pendulum, holding it over each square of paper and asking if this is the correct number for the upcoming drawing.

The future is not fixed and, because so many people are emotionally focused on the outcome of the lottery, this may make it difficult to obtain correct answers. But, if you do an experiment with guesses versus focused attempts to obtain information about the numbers from the etheric field, you will likely find that the pendulum results are superior to mere guesses.

The pendulum can, also, be used to communicate with spirits, similar to how a Ouija board is used for this purpose. Draw a semi-circle on a blank sheet of paper and place the letters, A to Z, the words "Yes" and "No," and the digits, zero to nine, at an equal distance around the edge of it. Position your pendulum in the center and ask it point to the answer to your question. For example, if you want to know the name of the spirit that is haunting a location, you can ask the pendulum to point to the first letter in the name, then the second, and so on.

Use the pendulum to find a lost article. There are different methods you may employ to do this. For example, physically go to each room and ask, "Is the object in this room?" Instead, you might draw a map of the house and hold the pendulum over each location represented and ask the same question. You might, also, make a list of each room in the house, then hold the pendulum over it and ask the question.

Always formulate your question, and then assume the mindset of an observer and allow the pendulum to give its answer. If you are having difficulty receiving accurate answers, consider how you worded your question. The pendulum is an extension of your subconscious mind, which takes your wording very literally. Make sure your question is precise and unequivocal.

The ability to focus for, at least, short periods of time is important to accuracy with the pendulum. If you are still having difficulty, make sure you are sufficiently hydrated. If you are feeling tired or anxious, wait until you have rested and your mind is more serene and then try, again.

Dowsing is a natural ability everyone has and you should be able to do it in a matter of minutes, but if you would like to learn more about dowsing, the *American Society of Dowsers* is a nationwide organization that teaches people how to dowse. (www.dowsers.org) A similar organization exists in the U.K. (www.britishdowsers.org)

Using a pendulum, dowsing rod, or other method of dowsing is a way to get used to receiving information about all kinds of different frequencies. As you practice with your pendulum, take notice of how you feel whenever you obtain correct answers. Try to learn the difference between what a guess feels like and what real information coming to you from an outside source feels like.

Regularly employing this skill helps to improve your higher intuition and improves claircognitive abilities. Every time you successfully dowse, you prove to yourself that you have the ability to interpret frequencies outside the ordinary physical range, thus breaking down the shared illusion of common reality.

Organizations that Study and Encourage Psychic Abilities

It is beneficial to be around other people who have psychic abilities or who are interested in further developing them. For this reason, you may find it helpful to join a psychic research group, a paranormal research society, or ghost hunting group. Joining an organization whether small or large, formal or informal, will surround you with supportive people with whom you can share your experiences.

Ghost hunting groups have become very popular in recent years and it is very likely that there is a local group near you, even if you live in a very small town. If there isn't, place a local advertisement and form your own investigation group. Begin by investigating haunted locations using basic equipment, such as cameras, audio and video recorders, and electromagnetic frequency detectors.

One of the oldest and most respected paranormal research organizations in the U.S. is the *Mutual U.F.O. Network* (M.U.F.O.N.). Their research into unexplained aerial phenomena crosses over into parapsychology and esoteric science. They offer a training program for field agents that can help you become an excellent paranormal investigator.

Spiritualist churches are good places to get exposure to séances, psychometry, and other kinds of psychic readings. These organizations teach people how to become psychics and mediums, and are good places to get started. They are not Christian organizations, but like most old, authoritative organizations they tend to be dogmatic.

Psychical research organizations, both small and large, exist in various places throughout the U.S., the U.K., and other Western countries. In the U.S., the major organization is the *American Society for Psychical Research* (www.aspr.com), although there are smaller research organizations in some cities. In the U.K., the main organization is the *Society for Psychical Research*. (www.spr.ac.uk) There are similar organizations in many other countries.

These are all places to find like-minded people, receive education and training, and participate in organized events.

If you don't live near one of these organizations and you'd still like to have an experience with an organized group, check your local phone book, or do a local online search for a paranormal research group or a metaphysical store.

Do not despair if you cannot find a ready-made group of people who share your interest. The best research groups often consist of two or three good friends who agree to meet regularly to experiment.

If you have a broader circle of friends who might be interested, begin by throwing a psychic party and determine from there who would be interested in more regular meetings and what kinds of experiments you would like to engage in. You can create a mediumship development circle or engage in a range of different psychic development exercises at your meetings.

The most successful psychic development circles in history consisted of family members and close friends, who met weekly for a common purpose.

If you are not especially social, don't worry. You can do a great deal on your own, especially if you have a quiet place and some time to devote to study and practice.

Conduct Your Own Parapsychological Experiments

Zerner cards were designed by Karl Werner and first used in parapsychological experiments in the 1930s. They are the classic E.S.P. test cards featuring five distinct images: A square; a circle; wavy lines; a star; and a plus sign. These cards can be used to help you hone your skills as a clairvoyant.

Obtain a deck of *Zerner* cards and shuffle them thoroughly. With the cards face down, count out 25 cards. On a blank sheet of paper, number down the page from 1 to 25. Begin with the first card on the top and without looking at it, close your eyes and clairvoyantly see the image on the card. Sometimes the image will not come quickly and you will be inclined to guess, but resist this temptation. Write down the image you see on the first card. Then look at the card to see if your answer is correct and mark it accordingly on the same line. Then move to the second card and repeat this procedure until you reach the end of the pile.

When you have finished, calculate the number of correct answers. When the cards are used for E.S.P. testing, a score of 10 out of 25 is considered good. But your goal is not so much to prove that you have such abilities as it is to improve the abilities you have.

Do not be disappointed if you don't get more than a few correct, at first. Be patient and concentrate on what happens, what you see, and how you see it when you get a correct answer. You will discover that there is a particular feeling or means by which the image presents itself to your inner vision. Remember this as you practice and try to repeat your successes. As you do, you will see an improved score. But, more importantly, you will be learning the difference between a guess and a clairvoyant experience.

You may, also, use the cards with a partner. Shuffle the cards and have a friend visualize them, one after another, in succession. As this is done, one by one, you will receive the image your friend is sending you and interpret the signals to form an inner vision. Write down each image in succession and when you have gone through all of the cards, stop and calculate the number of correct answers.

Online *Zerner* card tests, such as those at www.psychicscience.org, are very useful, too. The most important thing to remember when using these cards for psychic development is to focus on learning how your mind works to interpret signals on a frequency range other than the physical. The procedure you go through in obtaining the results is more important than your score. The score is only a means of measuring your progress.

Spirit Communication Devices

One of the greatest obstacles to increasing your higher psychic abilities is an inability to release, from the subconscious mind, the culturally conditioned disbelief in psychic abilities. Seeing is truly believing, especially when there are other witnesses.

The following is excerpted from the book, *How to Communicate with Spirits: Séances, Ouija Boards and Summoning,* by Angela Kaelin:

> *A number of different devices have been developed and continue to be improved upon by an unknown number of independent experimenters.*
>
> *They are based on devices like the Psychophone, George Meek's "Spiricom" Device, and Frank Sumpter's design, called "Frank's Box" or the "Ghost Box."*
>
> *The Frank's Box resembles a radionics machine (a magneto-electric computer that emits very low radio-like waves for healing purposes), although it emits audible sounds. It is tuned in a similar fashion by a psychically sensitive person. Plans for these and similar devices are scattered around the web along with videos of people using them. Search on-line for "Frank's Box Plans" or "Ghost Box Plans."*
>
> *Other technology has, also, been used in spirit communication. Common devices like recorders are used to record Electric Voice Phenomena (E.V.P.), but this is limiting because there is a delay in communication because the recording must be played back to be*

heard. Sometimes the messages are not recognized until after the opportunity for communication has passed.

When a person's mind is quiet and receptive, spirits sometimes use telephones to communicate. While it's not the most commonly reported type of communication, some people receive phone calls from deceased relatives or previously unknown spirits. The spirits often have a reason for making contact. They may have something they want to say to a living relative or they have interests in common with the contactee. Living people who have an interest in healing or science have been contacted by the spirits of departed healers and scientists.

Some people have received communications through the television, especially analog signals that produce "snow" or static. The static or "white noise" produced by an ordinary radio or even an electric fan has been used by spirits to form their voices and speak to the living.

Spirits commonly manifest as orbs or more distinct ghostly formations in photographs and videos. They can be seen through the lens of the camera where you look through when you want to take a photograph, so they can be seen in real time in this way.

Once you are aware of their presence, you can address them either by speaking out loud or communicating with them silently. Very often, if you ask them to do something, like pose for a picture or follow you, they will oblige.

Acquiring a spirit communication device or building one of your own and experimenting with white noise and E.V.P.s helps you to overcome the lingering subconscious programming of disbelief in psychic abilities.

Experimenting with ghost photography helps you to realize that things really are happening on frequency ranges outside your ordinary physical range of perception. With a digital camera or digital video recorder you will be able to see through the view finder that which you cannot see with your normal vision. This is a good way to make first contact with spirits of the deceased. By using the camera to help you know that they are present, you can begin a dialogue with them.

By doing these experiments you become more comfortable with the idea of clairvoyance and clairaudience. It begins to seem more natural and normal to you the more you do it. Eventually, you don't need any devices to receive very precise information.

Psychometry in Practice

Psychometry is the ability to interpret the frequencies that are imprinted upon an object to obtain information in the form of strong impressions, images, sounds, and other sensations.

Extensions of this ability include places that give a strong impression. Therefore, it is important to quietly and meditatively spend time in historically significant places and try to receive impressions from the environment.

Make an appointment to spend some time in known power centers like Sedona, Arizona, Machu Picchu, Peru, and Stonehenge. Visit art galleries and museums that have items with strong impressions in them. Bring your camera to record your experience. Go alone or with a friend who shares your interests.

Make a point of visiting places that have a special vibrations such as cemeteries, historical places, old battle fields, and places of quiet, untouched, natural beauty. Visit shrines and other locations that have been the scene of spiritual visitations and miracles.

The practice of psychometry, also, extends to people. Keep this in mind when you shake hands with people, especially those you are meeting for the first time. It is upon these initial moments of contact that you are likely to receive the strongest impressions, even images and internal monologues.

To increase your ability to read the frequencies associated with objects, experiment with items belonging to friends. Conduct an experiment at a party by collecting a small, significant object from each person in the room and placing them in a basket.

Take turns practicing psychometry by having someone choose an item from the basket. Have the psychic readers hold the object, close their eyes and tell what they see, hear, or what thoughts they have associated with the object. Do this in succession until there are no more unread objects left in the basket.

Afterward, the owners of each item can tell the story attached to the object they put into the basket so you can see how accurate the readings were.

Chapter 10
Journaling and Keeping Records

When you make the decision to improve your advanced psychic abilities, start a journal for this purpose. It can be a special, beautiful book or a common spiral notebook. This is up to you.

You don't have to make a commitment to writing in it every day, just keep it handy and record in it whatever you do that pertains to psychic development.

For example, when you make a change in your diet, write this down along with the date. Make a statement about what you are eliminating or adding to your diet. If you experiment with particular herbs or crystals, make a note about how you proceeded with this and when you began the experiment. When you end your experiment, record the results.

When you have a spontaneous psychic experience, write this down along with all supporting facts and details of the situation. If you have a premonition or a vision that provides verifiable information, this is important.

If you have a particularly colorful or vivid dream, write down as many details about your dream as you can. Some dreams are premonitions and, if you write down the date and details, you have proof for yourself and others when the dream yields correct information about a future event. It's one thing to tell people about a dream and have it come true, but when you have it written in a book, you can point to the information and it is more difficult to deny.

If you have an artistic inclination, make sketches of landscapes and entities you see whether in dreams or during waking hours.

If you conduct séances, tarot readings, or other kinds of psychic sessions, record the details of these events in the same way. Write down every significant detail you can think of. Include information about astrological timing, solar flares, moon phases, and weather conditions.

Atmospheric Conditions and Astrological Timing

Atmospheric and planetary influences may affect your advanced psychic abilities. The phase of the moon, the electromagnetic activity in the earth caused by sunspot activity, the weather, and planetary alignments are some factors acknowledged by ancient and modern researchers to have an effect on paranormal activity. Therefore, as a reference for yourself, you may want to take note of these conditions in relation to any psychic experience you have.

For example, some people believe their clairvoyant powers are stronger at the time of a full moon or at the new moon, however, your own experience may differ. It's possible that you may find that it has no verifiable influence on your abilities, at all. But noting these details in your records may help you get a more complete picture of how your own advanced psychic abilities function.

The following is excerpted from the book, *How to Communicate with Spirits: Séances, Ouija Boards and Summoning,* by Angela Kaelin:

Libra Time

Local Sidereal Time (LST) is used by astrologers to keep track of planetary movements. Paranormal researchers have found that their experiments render more accurate results at a Local Sidereal Time of 13:30. It is the time of Galactic Center Rising. It is, also, referred to as "Libra Time" because the constellation Libra is at 24 degrees and almost directly overhead.

This conclusion is documented by Dr. James P. Spottiswoode and Edwin C. May in, "Anomalous Cognition Effect Size: Dependence on Sidereal Time and Solar Wind Parameters," in "The Journal for Scientific Exploration." See this and other documentation at: http://www.jsasoc.com/library.html.

Determine your Local Sidereal Time by using a LST calculator or a sidereal clock. Free smart phone applications and software are now available on-line for this purpose.

Calculate your Local Sidereal Time using your longitude at: http://tycho.usno.navy.mil/sidereal.html.

Dates and Sabbats

Certain dates may prove more favorable for spirit communication. The following are Sabbats or traditional holy days. The actual time of each occasion may vary by a day in any given year, so consult an astrological calendar, a witches' almanac, or a farmers' almanac to be precise.

Halloween or Samhain: *October 31st*
Yule or Winter Equinox: *December 21st*
Imbolc: *February 2nd*
Ostara or Spring Equinox: *March 21st*
Beltane or May Day: *April 30th*
Litha or Summer Equinox: *June 21st*
Lughnassadh: *August 2nd*
Mabon or Autumn Equinox: *September 21st*

Of course, Halloween is traditionally believed to be the best time for the successful practice of advanced psychic abilities.

Take note of any of these factors in your journals and records to help you determine if there is any effect from them or not. If you find that your endeavors are consistently more successful under certain circumstances, then you have a foundation for future successful experiments

Chapter 11
Pitfalls to Be Aware Of

The Dangers of Sharing Your Abilities or Information with the Wrong People

There are certain people you should generally not talk to about your psychic experiences. In particular, these are police and other law enforcement agents, doctors, psychiatrists, and other mainstream medical professionals.

It is true that under special circumstances some police departments make use of psychics, but often the psychic is already friends with someone who bothers to follow up on a "hunch." There are always risks involved in approaching the police. You could be accused of making a false report, interfering or, worse, being involved in the crime, if you know too much about it.

The following story illustrates why you should not share your experiences with medical professionals:

After a traumatic experience that put her boyfriend in the hospital emergency room, a young woman observed that a staff member, who entered the room, had a demonic appearance. She mentioned this to a physician, who wanted her to undergo a psychiatric evaluation and would probably have put her on dangerous psychiatric medication. Fortunately, she mentioned this to a psychic friend who was familiar with this experience. The friend advised her to recant her story. The next time the young woman saw the doctor, she denied seeing anything unusual and the doctor dropped the idea of drugging her and possibly committing her to a psychiatric ward.

Mainstream medical professionals are in business to stay in business and make money. One way they do this is by convincing perfectly healthy people that they are sick and putting them on addictive drugs. The psychiatric medications that doctors prescribe are not only dangerous to your physical and mental health, but they actually open people up to demonic possession. In many cases, they cause people to engage in the very behavior the drugs are supposed to prevent, such as committing suicide or homicide.

If you have the ability to see and hear what is in another person's mind, it is often wise to keep this information to yourself, even if you aren't in the presence of a law enforcement agent or medical professional. The exception, of course, is if you are a professional psychic or fortune teller, in which case it is your job to tell people what you can see.

But, in the course of day-to-day events, you may encounter people who are duplicitous, criminals, or in some other way dangerous or living double lives. Very sophisticated psychic abilities are a frightening prospect to people who have a lot of secrets. If you reveal what you know, you may open yourself up to negative consequences in an attempt to silence you.

So, only share your experiences with open-minded people who are not in a position to harm you or use you in some way.

Receiving Unreliable or Suspicious Information

Not all of the information you receive by extrasensory means is going to be accurate. In most cases it is not easily verified. Nonetheless, you would be wise to analyze any information you receive just as you would if you received it from a living person or some other physical source.

Occasionally, you may have a natural clairvoyant or clairaudient experience, which you interpret incorrectly. This is a case of receiving good information, but ascribing something to it based on some misconception you hold.

For instance, just because you are able to see a person's spirit guide and it is not especially dark doesn't mean the person is good or highly spiritual. It could still be a possessing entity. Some look very human and are capable of shifting their appearance. Don't make wrong assumptions about a person or ascribe any special qualities to them based on something like this.

Some types of information are suspicious. For example, sometimes people report certain types of channeling experiences wherein they are given revelations, by means of voices or visions, that the world is coming to an end. They are sometimes told that humans are responsible for the impending destruction of the planet, but extra-terrestrials are here to save a select few.

This is the type of subtle electronic transmission that is received by some channelers from a psychological operation broadcast calling itself Ashtar Command or The Galactic Federation of Light. It appears to be some kind of mind manipulation experiment. The people who receive these transmissions are usually very adamant about the veracity of the information they have been given because of the extraordinary means by which they received it. They are convinced that their ability to receive the transmission makes them special and the message they receive is very comforting. Furthermore, others who are mentally attuned to the frequency on which these messages are broadcast are receiving similar transmissions, which makes the hoax seem all the more convincing.

Generally speaking, messages from peaceful aliens or abduction experiences involving entities that look like cartoon characters are an indication that the person is a mind control subject. To such people, their perceptions of these experiences are real, but in reality they are unwitting victims of an experiment of some kind perpetrated on them against their will by other human beings.

Similarly, sometimes people receive messages they believe are from extraterrestrials or god, when in fact they are victims of organized gang stalking and electronic harassment. Such victims are broadcast personalized messages according to their pre-existing belief systems.

For example, those with pre-existing Christian programming receive messages which they are convinced are from God or Jesus. Non-religious people or New Agers receive messages they believe are from benevolent aliens or angels. Sometimes the people figure out that they are being hoaxed, but they still have difficulty convincing the people around them who cannot hear the messages. Many of these unfortunate people fall into the hands of medical or psychiatric professionals who drug and sometimes even temporarily imprison them.

These are examples of occult technology based, in part, on the esoteric science of the Theosophists. It has a lot in common with quantum mechanics, however, it is not the science that is taught in universities. This information has been hoarded by governments ostensibly for defense purposes, although it appears that the reasons may be far more insidious. Mind influencing technology, like the Lida Machine, is decades old, much of it dating back to the old Soviet Union, but it has become increasingly sophisticated in recent years.

Although the problem of electronic harassment is receiving more public attention and awareness, it is still fairly unknown. But it is important for you to know that it exists, so you can distinguish such experiences from genuine spirit communication.

Chapter 12
Signs that Your Abilities are Developing

As your advanced psychic abilities develop and expand, you may experience an entire shift in your perspective on the world. This can be disconcerting and disorienting. You may feel as if the rug has been pulled out from under your feet.

You may even experience some of the symptoms associated with anxiety such as difficulty sleeping, a feeling of some impending fate, and even heart palpitations.

Your dreams may become more vivid and realistic. Your subconscious mind may begin dredging up old memories. You may receive visitations from deceased relatives or maybe even ancestors whom you've never met.

You may experience either a sudden increase or decrease in energy. In the latter case, you may seem to require more sleep than usual and find yourself in waking dream states at odd times. In the former case, you may have bursts of energy and expanded creativity and inspiration.

You may have the sense the someone is trying to get your attention. When you are in bed, it may shake from side to side as if it is being pushed. You may have the sensation of cobwebs on your face or experience the sensation of being touched by an invisible hand. You may even receive strange phone calls or other electronic communications, which is a method some spirits like to use to send messages to those they choose to speak to.

Before you begin to see and hear presences, you may have a strong sense of them around you. Do not edit or deny this experience. When you sense a presence, engage it. Ask it to speak to you. Allow it to use you as a channel or medium and give it permission to do so, either silently or aloud.

Another common effect of expanding ability is the sense that you can see through people. You seem to be able to see the true person or the soul manifestation.

These experiences only seem extraordinary to us because they have been intentionally removed from the collective reality. But they are as natural as breathing, walking, and talking. As your abilities continue to expand, you will begin to understand this beyond the meaning any mere words can convey. It will become a part of you and a part of your everyday life.

This unsettling period of development eventually passes, and you will emerge on the other side a different person with a broader understanding of how the world really is.

Chapter 13
Final Words of Encouragement

Most people like to go with the flow and be a part of the crowd. They don't want to be seen as different because they fear ridicule or worse. It takes a lot of courage to be different from others and to admit, even to yourself, that you see, hear, and know things that other people do not.

Most often, we are our own barrier to these abilities because we harbor a subconscious fear of them. But it is always better to face the truth than deny it. Once you accept that you have these natural abilities, even if others cannot, it is in your best interest to develop them to their fullest extent because it gives you an advantage in life.

One way to accelerate your progress is to simply ask to know something or be shown something. This is very effective. It doesn't matter whom you ask. You do not have to address your question to a particular entity. Then, quiet your mind. Silence your inner monologue or your "chattering monkey" and wait for the answer to come.

Keep the idea of reading people on the etheric, astral, or mental planes in mind when you first meet new people. In the initial seconds of meeting someone, making eye contact, and even physical contact by shaking hands, you have the best opportunity to receive information about them through clairaudience or clairvoyance.

Continue to read about psychic experiences and psychic development. It is important to set aside a little time, once in a while, to experiment with your developing skills, but it is equally important, if not more so, to keep your mind on the idea of attempting to expand your abilities all the time, in every situation.

The archaic meaning of the word, "will," is "to want" or "to desire" something. It is this exercise of your will or desire in day-to-day life that is critical to developing your psychic abilities to their utmost. Strive every day, whether you are in your normal work environment, going about routine tasks, interacting with friends or strangers, to maintain a high level of sensory awareness. This takes a strong will and a focused desire to strain your sensory abilities just a little beyond what you think you are presently capable of.

Expect the unexpected and do not edit what you see. If you saw something unusual, accept that you did. Often people will edit out information that doesn't fit with their preconceived notions of how the world is. Remember, the commonly perceived physical reality is programmed by the television, popular culture, religion, and the people around you who are involved in the same things. Developing advanced psychic abilities naturally takes you outside that common, artificially created reality.

Try to let go of false beliefs. Do not let religious beliefs or other restrictions dictate what you believe. Instead, let your experience and your research be your guide.

As you become increasingly aware of your abilities and it comes to the point where you can no longer remain in any stage of denial about it, many old structures of belief will probably be knocked down, whether you are ready or not. They will come down like the walls of a prison in your mind.

The End

References

1. Powell, A.E., *The Etheric Double: The Health Aura of Man,* The Theosophy Library, 1925.
2. Whitehouse, Dr. David, BBC News Online Science Editor, "Library of Alexandria Discovered, Wednesday," *BBC,* May 12, 2004. Retrieved February 15, 2012. Retrieved 3/5/2012.
   http://news.bbc.co.uk/2/hi/science/nature/3707641.stm
3. Morton, Chris and Ceri Louise Thomas, *The Mystery of the Crystal Skulls: A Real Life Detective Story of the Ancient World,* Bear & Co., July 1998.
4. Ostrander, Sheila and Lynn Schroeder, *Psychic Discoveries Behind the Iron Curtain,* Bantam, 1971.
5. Sommer, Charles, *The Next Step with Spirit: Extraordinary Events that Happen to Ordinary People,* DeVorss & Company, 1996. P. 53.
6. Strassman, Rick, *DMT: The Spirit Molecule: A Doctor's Revolutionary Research into the Biology of Near-Death and Mystical Experiences,* Park Street Press, 2000.
7. Arthur, James, *Mushrooms and Mankind: The Impact of Mushrooms on Human Consciousness and Religion,* The Book Tree, May 2003.
8. Hudson, David, *Superconductivity and Modern Alchemy.* Transcribed from video tapes recorded by The Eclectic Viewpoint on February 10 and 11, 1995. Retrieved 3/5/2012.
   http://www.rexresearch.com/ormes/hudsnlec.htm

9. Besant, Annie and C.W. Leadbeater, *Thought Forms,* The Theosophical Publishing House, London 1901. (The original version with color plates may be found at Gutenberg.org.)

Bibliography

Arthur, James. *Mushrooms and Mankind: The Impact of Mushrooms on Human Consciousness and Religion,* The Book Tree, May 2003.

Besant, Annie and C.W. Leadbeater. *Thought Forms,* The Theosophical Publishing House, London 1901. (The original version with color plates may be found at Gutenberg.org.)

Blavatsky, Helena Petrovna, *The Secret Doctrine,* Volumes 1 & 2, London, 1888.

Cayce, Edgar and Hugh Lynn Cayce, *Edgar Cayce on Atlantis,* Grand Central Publishing, April 1988.

Cheiro, *Palmistry for All,* G.P. Putnam's Sons, 1916. (www.gutenberg.org)

Crowley, Aleister, *Book 4,* Ordo Templi Orientis, 1913.

DiGregorio, Sophia, *Traditional Witches' Formulary and Potion-making Guide: Recipes for Magical Oils, Powders and Other Potions,* Winter Tempest Books, 2012.

Eden, Donna, *The Energy Medicine Kit,* Sounds True, April 2005.

Leadbeater, C.W., Clairvoyance, London, Theosophical Publishing Society, 1903.

Powell, A.E., *The Etheric Double, The Health Aura of Man,* The Theosophy Library, 1925, 1968.

Powell, A.E., *The Mental Body,* The Theosophy Library, 1927.

Strassman, Rick, *DMT: The Spirit Molecule: A Doctor's Revolutionary Research into the Biology of Near-Death and Mystical Experiences,* Park Street Press, December 2000.

Kaelin, Angela, *How to Read the Tarot for Fun, Profit and Psychic Development,* Winter Tempest Books, 2010.

Kaelin, Angela, *Magical Healing: How to Use Your Mind to Heal Yourself and Others,* Winter Tempest Books, 2011.

Kaelin, Angela, *How to Communicate with Spirits: Séances, Ouija Boards and Summoning,* Winter Tempest Books, 2011.

Ostrander, Sheila and Lynn Schroeder, *Psychic Discoveries Behind the Iron Curtain,* Bantam, 1971.

Puharich, Andrija, *The Sacred Mushroom: Key to the Door of Eternity,* Doubleday, 1974.

Saint-Germain, C. de, *Practice of Palmistry,* Newcastle Publishing Company, 1973.

Strassman, Rick, *DMT: The Spirit Molecule: A Doctor's Revolutionary Research into the Biology of Near-Death and Mystical Experiences,* Park Street Press, 2000.

Sui, Choa Kok, *Pranic Healing,* Red Wheel Weiser, June 1990.

Stein, Diane, *Essential Reiki: A Complete Guide to an Ancient Healing Art,* Crossing Press, April 1995.

Wasson, Gordon, *Soma: Divine Mushroom of Immortality,* Harcourt, April 1972.

BECOME A PATRON OF SOPHIA DIGREGORIO USING BITCOIN AND ALTCOINS

For more details about our Bitcoin and altcoin patronage program, please, read the free ebook, *The Occult Files of Sophia diGregorio Bitcoin and Altcoins Patronage Program: How to Join Our Cryptocurrency-based Patronage Program and Why We are Doing Things This Way*, which is available at the following websites:

Traditional Witchcraft and Occultism Wordpress Blog:
www.traditionalwitchcraftandoccultism.wordpress.com

The Occult Files of Sophia diGregorio Wordpress Blog:
www.occultfilesofsophiadigregorio.wordpress.com

Psychic Powers and Magic Spells:
www.psychic-powers-and-magic-spells.weebly.com

Winter Tempest Books at Webs:
www.wintertempestbooks.webs.com

To join our cryptocurrency-based patronage program, please, contact one of our administrators:

Max Goddard: MaxGoddard@protonmail.com
Kipp Kelsey: KippKelsey@tutamail.com

MORE WINTER TEMPEST BOOKS

If you enjoyed this book, you might enjoy other Winter Tempest Books:

All Natural Dental Remedies: Herbs and Home Remedies to Heal Your Teeth & Naturally Restore Tooth Enamel by Angela Kaelin

Black Magic for Dark Times: Spells of Revenge and Protection by Angela Kaelin

The Devil's Grimoire: A System of Psychic Attack by Moribus Mortlock

Grimoire of Santa Muerte: Spells and Rituals of Most Holy Death, the Unofficial Saint of Mexico (Santa Muerte Series) (Volume 1) by Sophia diGregorio

Grimoire of Santa Muerte, Vol. 2: Altars, Meditations, Divination and Witchcraft Rituals for Devotees of Most Holy Death (Santa Muerte Series) (Volume 2) by Sophia diGregorio

How to Communicate with Spirits: Séances, Ouija Boards and Summoning by Angela Kaelin

How to Read the Tarot for Fun, Profit and Psychic Development for Beginners and Advanced Readers by Angela Kaelin

How to Write Your Own Spells for Any Purpose and Make Them Work by Sophia diGregorio

Magical Healing: How to Use Your Mind to Heal Yourself and Others by Angela Kaelin

Natural Remedies for Reversing Gray Hair: Nutrition and Herbs for Anti-aging and Optimum Health by Thomas W. Xander

Practical Black Magic: How to Hex and Curse Your Enemies by Sophia diGregorio

Spells for Money and Wealth by Angela Kaelin

The Traditional Witches' Book of Love Spells by Angela Kaelin

Traditional Witches' Formulary and Potion-making Guide: Recipes for Magical Oils, Powders and Other Potions by Sophia diGregorio

What's Next After Wicca? Non-Wiccan Occult Practices and Traditional Witchcraft by Sophia diGregorio

Traditional Witches' History of the Occult Banking System: How Witches and Occultists Can Use Bitcoin and Altcoins for Privacy and Anti-Discrimination by Sophia diGregorio

The Occult Files of Sophia diGregorio: The Public Monologues of 2018 by Sophia diGregorio

ORDER OUR BOOKS WITH CRYPTOCURRENCY

To place an order for Winter Tempest Books using Bitcoin, Monero, Litecoin, Dogecoin, and other preferred altcoins, please, contact:

Kipp Kelsey: KippKelsey@tutamail.com

Max Goddard: MaxGoddard@protonmail.com

SOPHIA DIGREGORIO

SOPHIA DIGREGORIO'S DONATION CODES

Donate to the author:

Monero (XMR):
41wVxhAQchuESryqAQgnyhY7Qv4McnFrFZ6Sb
9ue16AdJzmGUMuBY6zP7cZ1JBG7nVfqJRUqW
zDBhayebZwae93pNkyFnMm

Bitcoin (BTC):
196qNENpoe8DGCt8mHYcm2xZ3oKZSxxyvq

Dogecoin (DOGE):
DBNNCYZe6WWPFZokjd933bm2eHLd9gAXzy

Litecoin (LTC):
La8aBs7BPVwP87tmKH9ggL1bVuoq2x866W

Dash (DASH):
XwTZaBxDSAxnAif3SWrkMUPhGSYXet5MpG

Bitcoin Cash (BCH):
14merNRUCMBHVJUDxb3q2ktdypUxiq4Qvu

Bitcoin Gold (BTG):
GRwsULUvqeHwCJ9V14J21b1GgS25KSz6S9

Zcash (ZEC):
t1f57jkSeiTLYMC1wcEWYu8BCLmRMDnfBmp

DISCLAIMERS

The author and publisher of this book has used her best efforts in preparing this document. The author of this book makes no representation or warranties with respect to the accuracy, applicability, fitness or completeness of the contents of this document and disclaims any warranties expressed or implied. The author is not a licensed medical, legal, or financial professional, and is not qualified to give medical, legal, or financial, or investment advice, and nothing in this document should be construed as such advice. Any substances, instruments, procedures, or information described in this book should not be used a substitute for treatment or advice from state approved, licensed medical authorities, attorneys, or financial advisors. Any medical, legal, or financial questions should be addressed to the proper authorities on such matters. The information in this book is not medical, legal, financial, or investment advice and should not be relied upon for such purposes.

Nothing in this book should be construed as incitement to dangerous or illegal acts and the reader is advised to be aware of and to heed and obey all pertinent laws in his or her city, state, country or other jurisdiction. The statements in this book have not been evaluated by any legal, licensed, or government entity, nor any representative thereof. The statements contained herein represent the author's legally protected opinion, represent her best work, and are complete and accurate to the best of her knowledge.

The material in this book is presented for informational and entertainment purposes only and anyone who uses any of the information in the book does so at his or her own risk with the understanding that the author cannot be held responsible for the consequences. The author or publisher is not responsible for your use of or experiences with of any websites, companies, software, services, or products mentioned herein. The author or publisher shall in no event be held liable for any losses or damages, including but not limited to special, incidental, consequential or other damages incurred by, arising from, or related to your reliance upon or use of this information.

FTC Disclaimer: The author has no connection to nor was paid by any brand or product described in this document with the exception of any other books mentioned which were written by the author or published by Winter Tempest Books.

Copyright: *How to Develop Advanced Psychic Abilities: Obtain Information about the Past, Present and Future Through Clairvoyance.*
Copyright © 2019 Sophia diGregorio All rights reserved.

License statement: This document contains material protected under copyright laws. Any unauthorized reprint, transmission or resale of this material without the express permission of the author is strictly prohibited. No part of this book may be used or reproduced in any manner whatsoever without written permission from the author except in the case of brief quotations embodied in critical articles and reviews.